SIXTH EDITION
GRAMMAR 3A
IN CONTEXT

SANDRA N. ELBAUM

NATIONAL GEOGRAPHIC LEARNING | CENGAGE Learning

Australia • Brazil • Mexico • Singapore • United Kingdom • United States

Grammar in Context 3A, Sixth Edition
Student Book
Sandra N. Elbaum

Publisher: Sherrise Roehr

Executive Editor: Laura Le Dréan

Development Editor: Claudi Mimó

Executive Marketing Manager: Ben Rivera

Senior Director, Production: Michael Burggren

Content Project Manager: Mark Rzeszutek

Manufacturing Planner: Mary Beth Hennebury

Interior Design: Brenda Carmichael

Compositor: SPi Global

Cover Design: Brenda Carmichael

Copyright © 2016, 2010, 2006 National Geographic Learning

ISBN 13: 978-1-305-07554-2

National Geographic Learning
20 Channel Center Street
Boston, Massachusetts 02210
USA

Cengage Learning is a leading provider of customized learning solutions with office locations around the globe, including Singapore, the United Kingdom, Australia, Mexico, Brazil, and Japan. Locate our local office at international.cengage.com/region

Cengage Learning products are represented in Canada by Nelson Education, Ltd.

Visit National Geographic Learning online at **ngl.cengage.com**
Visit our corporate website at **www.cengage.com**

Printed in the United States of America
Print Number: 01   Print Year: 2015

CONTENTS

GRAMMAR Verb Review
CONTEXT Language

GRAMMAR The Present Perfect and the Present Perfect Continuous
CONTEXT Risk

3

GRAMMAR Passive and Active Voice
CONTEXT The Movies

4

GRAMMAR The Past Continuous
The Past Perfect
The Past Perfect Continuous
CONTEXT Travel by Land, Sea, and Air

GRAMMAR Modals and Related Expressions
CONTEXT Technology

GRAMMAR Modals in the Past
CONTEXT U.S. Presidents and Elections

APPENDICES

GLOSSARY OF GRAMMATICAL TERMS

INDEX

ACKNOWLEDGMENTS

I am grateful to the team at National Geographic Learning/Cengage Learning for showing their faith in the *Grammar in Context* series by putting their best resources and talent into it. I would especially like to thank Laura Le Dréan for driving this series into an exciting, new direction. Her overall vision of this new edition has been a guiding light. I would also like to thank my development editor, Claudi Mimó, for managing the difficult day-to-day task of polishing and refining the manuscript toward its finished product. I would like to thank Dennis Hogan, Sherrise Roehr, and John McHugh for their ongoing support of *Grammar in Context* through its many editions.

I wish to acknowledge the immigrants, refugees, and international students I have known, both as a teacher and as a volunteer with refugee agencies. These people have increased my understanding of my own language and taught me to see life from another point of view. By sharing their observations, questions, and life stories, they have enriched my life enormously.

This new edition is dedicated to the millions of displaced people in the world. The United States is the new home of many refugees, who survived unspeakable hardships in Burundi, Rwanda, Iraq, Sudan, Burma, Bhutan, and other countries. Their resiliency in starting a new life and learning a new language is a tribute to the human spirit.
—*Sandra N. Elbaum*

Heinle would like to thank the following people for their contributions:

Dorothy S. Avondstondt, Miami Dade College—Wolfson Campus;

Pamela Ardizzone, Rhode Island College;

Patricia Bennett, Grossmont College;

Mariusz Bojarczuk, Bunker Hill Community College;

Rodney Borr, Glendale Community College;

Nancy Boyer, Golden West College;

Charles Brooks, Norwalk Community College;

Gabriela Cambiasso, Harold Washington College;

Julie Condon, St. Cloud State University;

Anne Damiecka, Lone Star College — CyFair;

Mohammed Debbagh, Virginia Commonwealth University;

Frank DeLeo, Broward College;

Jeffrey DiIuglio, Boston University Center for English Language and Orientation Programs;

Monique Dobbertin Cleveland, Los Angeles Pierce College;

Lindsey Donigan, Fullerton College;

Jennifer J. Evans, University of Washington;

Norm Evans, Brigham Young University—Hawaii;

David Gillham, Moraine Valley Community College;

Martin Guerra, Mountain View College;

Eric Herrera, Universidad Técnica Nacional;

Cora Higgins, Bunker Hill Community College;

Barbara Inerfeld, Rutgers University;

Barbara Jonckheere, California State University, Long Beach;

Gursharan Kandola, University of Houston;

Roni Lebrauer, Saddleback College;

Dr. Miriam Moore, Lord Fairfax Community College;

Karen Newbrun Einstein, Santa Rosa Junior College;

Stephanie Ngom, Boston University Center for English Language and Orientation Programs;

Charl Norloff, International English Center, University of Colorado Boulder;

Gabriella Nuttall, Sacramento City College;

Fernanda Ortiz, University of Arizona;

Dilcia Perez, Los Angeles City College;

Stephen Peridore, College of Southern Nevada;

Tiffany Probasco, Bunker Hill Community College;

Elizabeth Seabury, Bunker Hill Community College;

Natalia Schroeder, Long Beach City College;

Maria Spelleri, State College of Florida, Manatee-Sarasota;

Susan Stern, Irvine Valley College;

Vincent Tran, University of Houston;

Karen Vlaskamp, Northern Virginia Community College—Annandale;

Christie Ward, Intensive English Language Program, Central Connecticut State University;

Colin Ward, Lone Star College—North Harris;

Laurie A. Weinberg, J. Sargeant Reynolds Community College

A WORD FROM THE AUTHOR

My parents immigrated to the United States from Poland and learned English as a second language as adults. My sisters and I were born in the United States. My parents spoke Yiddish to us; we answered in English. In that process, my parents' English improved immeasurably. Such is the case with many immigrant parents whose children are fluent in English. They usually learn English much faster than others; they hear the language in natural ways, in the context of daily life.

Learning a language in context, whether it be from the home, from work, or from a textbook, cannot be overestimated. The challenge for me has been to find a variety of high-interest topics to engage the adult language learner. I was thrilled to work on this new edition of *Grammar in Context* for National Geographic Learning. In so doing, I have been able to combine exciting new readings with captivating photos to exemplify the grammar.

I have given more than 100 workshops at ESL programs and professional conferences around the United States, where I have gotten feedback from users of previous editions of *Grammar in Context*. Some teachers have expressed concern about trying to cover long grammar lessons within a limited time. While ESL is not taught in a uniform number of hours per week, I have heeded my audiences and streamlined the series so that the grammar and practice covered is more manageable. And in response to the needs of most ESL programs, I have expanded and enriched the writing component.

Whether you are a new user of *Grammar in Context* or have used this series before, I welcome you to this new edition.

Sandra N. Elbaum

For my loves
Gentille, Chimene, Joseph, and Joy

Grammar in Context presents grammar in interesting contexts that are relevant to students' lives and then recycles the language and context throughout every activity. Learners gain knowledge and skills in both grammar structures and topic areas.

New To This Edition

NATIONAL GEOGRAPHIC PHOTOGRAPHS
introduce lesson themes and draw learners into the context.

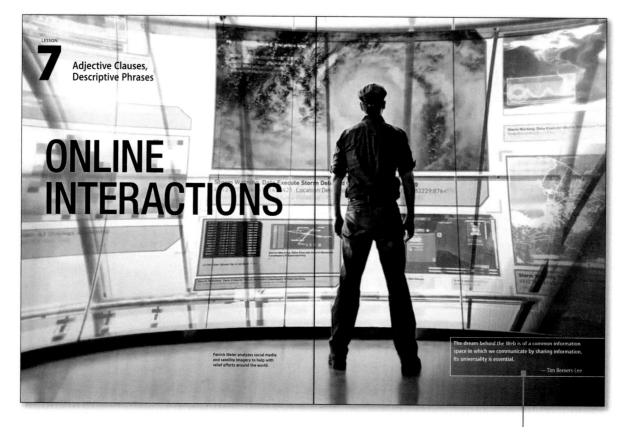

LESSON

7 Adjective Clauses, Descriptive Phrases

ONLINE INTERACTIONS

Patrick Meier analyzes social media and satellite imagery to help with relief efforts around the world.

The dream behind the Web is of a common information space in which we communicate by sharing information. Its universality is essential.

— Tim Berners-Lee

New To This Edition

EVERY LESSON OPENER
includes a quote from an artist, scientist, author, or thinker that helps students connect to the theme.

NEW AND UPDATED READINGS, many with National Geographic content, introduce the target grammar in context and provide the springboard for practice.

NEW LISTENING EXERCISES reinforce the grammar through natural spoken English.

The
LOST BOYS
of SUDAN

Sudanese refugees, and "Lost Boys" at a camp in Kenya

SUDAN
SOUTH SUDAN ETHIOPIA

🎧 **Read the following article. Pay special attention to the words in bold.**

Besides immigrants, the United States takes in thousands of refugees a year. The Lost Boys of Sudan were children, living in southern Sudan in the late 1980s, when their long and difficult journey to the United States began. **While** these young boys were in the field taking care of their cattle,[3] their villages were attacked. These children, mostly boys between the ages of 4 and 12, ran for their lives. **For** three months, they walked hundreds of miles **until** they reached Ethiopia. They survived by eating leaves, roots, and wild fruit.

During that time, many died of starvation[4] and disease or were eaten by wild animals. Those who reached Ethiopia stayed in refugee camps **until** 1991, when a war started in Ethiopia and the camps were closed. They ran again, back to Sudan and then to Kenya, where they stayed in refugee camps **for** almost ten years. Of the approximately 27,000 boys who fled Sudan, only 11,000 survived.

During their time in the refugee camp, they got some schooling and learned basic English. In 1999, the United Nations and the U.S. government agreed to resettle 3,800 Lost Boys in the United States.

When they arrived in the United States, many challenges awaited them. They had to learn a completely new way of life. Many things were new

for them: apartment living in a big city, strange foods, new technologies, and much more. **When** they saw an American supermarket for the first time, they were amazed by the amount of food. One boy was so surprised by the quantity of food in a supermarket that he asked if it was the palace of the king.

Agencies helped the Lost Boys with money for food and rent for a short time **until** they found jobs. **While** they were working, most of them enrolled in ESL classes. Now men, many have graduated from college and have started projects to help their villages back home. Peter Magai Bul, of Chicago, helped establish a school in his hometown. **While** he was studying for his college degree, Peter helped to raise funds for this school, which is currently educating over five hundred South Sudan students.

Although their future in the United States looks bright, **whenever** they think about their homeland, they are sad because so many of their family members and friends have died.

[3] *cattle:* cows, bulls, and oxen as a group
[4] *starvation:* the state of having no food, being extremely hungry

Connecting Ideas **257**

COMPREHENSION CHECK Based on the reading, tell if the statement is true (**T**) or false (**F**).

1. The Lost Boys were in a refugee camp in Ethiopia until they came to the U.S.
2. When their villages were attacked, the Lost Boys ran back home.
3. Some of the Lost Boys are helping their people in South Sudan.

9.3 Time Clauses and Phrases

Examples	Explanation
When their villages were attacked, the Lost Boys ran. Some young men will help their people back home **when** they finish college.	*When* means "at that time" or "immediately after that time." In a future sentence, we use the present in the time clause.
Whenever they think about their country, they are sad. **Whenever** they tell their story, Americans are amazed.	*Whenever* means "any time" or "every time."
They walked **until** they reached Ethiopia. They received money for a short time **until** they got jobs.	*Until* means "up to that time."
Peter has been a student **since** he came to the U.S. He has been working **(ever) since** he arrived in the U.S.	*Since* or *ever since* means "from that time in the past to the present." We use the present perfect or present perfect continuous in the main clause.
While they were taking care of their cattle, their villages were bombed. **As** they were coming to the U.S., they were thinking about their new life ahead.	We use *while* or *as* with a continuous action.
They walked **for** three months. They stayed in a refugee camp **for** many years.	We use *for* with an amount of time.
During the day, they walked. **During** their time in the refugee camp, they studied English.	We use *during* with a time such as *the day* or *summer,* or with a specific time period (*their time in Ethiopia, the month of August*) or an event (*the flight to the U.S.*).

EXERCISE 6 Fill in the blanks with *since, until, while, when, as, during, for,* or *whenever.* In some cases, more than one answer is possible.

1. The Lost Boys were very young ____when____ they left Sudan.

2. The Lost Boys walked _____ many months.

3. _____ their march to Ethiopia, many of them died.

4. They lived in Ethiopia _____ about four years.

258 Lesson 9

NEW REDESIGNED GRAMMAR CHARTS offer straightforward explanations and provide contextualized clear examples of the structure.

TEST/REVIEW

Use the sentence under each blank to form a noun clause. Answers may vary.

Two years ago, when I was eighteen, I didn't know ___what to do___ with my life. I had just
　　　　　　　　　　　　　　　　　　　　　　1. What should I do?

graduated from high school, and I couldn't decide _____.
　　　　　　　　　　　　　　　　　　　　　2. Should I go to college or not?

A neighbor of mine told me _____ and decided to
　　　　　　　　　　　　　3. I had the same problem when I was your age.

go to the U.S. for a year to work as an au pair. She asked me

_____. I told her _____. She told me
4. Have you ever heard of this program?　　　　　　5. I haven't.

_____ and _____
6. I lived with an American family for a year.　　　　7. My English has improved a lot.

I asked her _____. I was surprised to find out
　　　　　　8. How much will this program cost me?

_____. I asked her _____, and
9. You'll earn about $200 a week.　　　　　　　　　10. Is the work very hard?

she said _____ but _____.
　　　11. It is.　　　　　12. It is very rewarding.

When I told my parents _____, they told me
　　　　　　　　　　　　13. I am thinking about going to the U.S. for a year.

SUMMARY OF LESSON 10

Direct Statement or Question	Sentence with an Included Statement or Question	Explanation
She loves kids. She is patient.	I know **that she loves kids.** I'm sure **that she is patient.**	A noun clause is used as an included statement.
Is the baby sick? What does the baby need?	I don't know **if the baby is sick.** I'm not sure **what the baby needs.**	A noun clause is used as an included question.
What should I do with a crying baby? Where can I find a babysitter?	I don't know **what to do with a crying baby.** Can you tell me **where to find a babysitter?**	An infinitive can replace *should* or *can.*
You know more than you think you do. Do you have children?	Dr. Spock said, **"You know more than you think you do." "Do you have children?"** asked the doctor.	An exact quote is used to report what someone has said or asked.
Do your kids watch Sesame Street? I will teach my son to drive.	She asked me **if my kids watched** Sesame Street. She said **that she would tea** her son to drive.	A noun clause is used in reported
Trust yourself. Don't give the baby candy.	He told us **to trust ourselv** He told me **not to give the l candy.**	

Punctuation with Noun Clauses	
I know where he lives.	Period at
Do you know where he lives?	Question noun clau
He said, "I like you."	Comma at Period be
"I like you," he said.	Quotation the final
He asked, "What do you want?"	Comma a quote. Qu
"What do you want?" he asked.	Quotation before th

PART 2 Editing Practice

Some of the shaded words and phrases have mistakes. Find the mistakes and correct them. If the shaded words are correct, write *C.*

　　　　　　　　　　　　　　　　　　　　　　　　　　　　　that
　　When I was fourteen years old, I told my parents ~~what~~ I wanted to work as a babysitter, but they
　　　　　　　　　　　　　　　　　　　　　　　　　1.
C
told me that I was too young. At that time, they told me that they will pay me $1 an hour to help
2.　　3.　　　　　　　　　　　　　　　　　　　　　　　　　　　　　4.
with my little brother. A few times they asked me could I watch him when they went out. They
　　　　　　　　　　　　　　　　　　　　5.
always told me call them immediately in case of a problem. They told me don't watch TV or text my
　　　　　　　　6.　　　　　　　　　　　　　　　　　　　　　　7.
friends while I was working as a babysitter. They always told me that I have done a good job.
　　　　　　　　　　　　　　　　　　　　　　　　　　　　8.
　　When I was fifteen, I got a few more responsibilities, like preparing small meals. They always
told that I should teach my brother about good nutrition. I asked them whether I could get more
9.　10.　　　　　　　　　　　　　　　　　　　　　　　　　　　11.
money because I had more responsibilities, and they agreed. I asked them if I can buy something
　　　　　　　　　　　　　　　　　　　　　　　　　　　　12.
new with my earnings. My parents said, "Of course."
　　　　　　　　　　　　　13.
　　When I turned eighteen, I started working for my neighbors, who have three children. The
neighbors asked me had I gotten my driver's license yet. When I said yes, they were pleased because
　　　　　　　　14.　　　　　　　　　　　　　　　15.
I could drive the kids to different places. I never realized how hard was it to take care of so many
　　　　　　　　　　　　　　　　　　　　　　　　　　16.
kids. As soon as we get in the car, they ask, "Are we there yet?" They think so we should arrive
　　　　　　　　　　　　　　17.　　　　　　　　　　　　18.
immediately. When they're thirsty, they ask me to buy them soda, but I tell them what it is healthier
　　　　　　　　　　　　　19.　　　　　　　　　　　20.　　21.
to drink water. They always tell, "In our house we drink soda." I don't understand why do their
　　　　　　　　　22.　　　　　　　　　　　　　　　　　　　　23.
　　　　　　w whether to follow the rules of my house or
　　　　　24.
　　　　　rents told me not to say anything about their
　　　　　26.
　　　　　lthy habits by example.
　　　　　hildren. I hope that I will be as good a mom to
　　　　　　　　　　　28.

　　　　when you were a child. Explain what the

　　　　u or encouraged you when you were a child.

　　　　Edit your writing from Part 3.

Noun Clauses 313

WRITING

PART 1 Editing Advice

1. Use *that* or nothing to introduce an included statement. Don't use *what.*
　　　　　　that
　I know ~~what~~ she is a good driver.

2. Use statement word order in an included question.
　　　　　　　　　　he is
　I don't know how fast ~~is he~~ driving.

3. We *say* something. We *tell* someone something.
　　　told
　He ~~said~~ me that he wanted to go home.
　　　said
　He ~~told~~, "I want to go home."

4. Use *tell* or *ask,* not *say,* to report an imperative. Follow *tell* and *ask* with an object.
　　　　　　　told
　Dr. Spock ~~said~~ parents to trust themselves.
　　　　　　　　me
　My son asked ⌃ to give him the car keys.

5. Don't use *to* after *tell.*
　She told ~~to~~ me that she wanted to be a teacher.

6. Use *if* or *whether* to introduce an included *yes/no* question. Use statement word order.
　　　　　　　　whether
　I don't know ⌃ teenagers understand the risks while driving.
　　　　　　　　if I should
　I can't decide ~~should I~~ let my daughter get her driver's license.

7. Follow the rule of sequence of tenses when the main verb is in the past.
　　　　　　　　　　　　　　would
　Last year my father said that he ~~will~~ teach me how to drive, but he didn't.

8. Don't use *so* before a noun clause.
　I think ~~so~~ raising children is the best job.

9. Use an infinitive to report an imperative.
　　　　　　　　　　　to
　My parents told me ⌃ drive carefully.
　　　　　　　　　　　not to
　My parents told me ⌃ ~~don't~~ text while driving.

312 Lesson 10

Enhanced For This Edition!

END-OF-LESSON ACTIVITIES
help learners review and apply the
target grammar to writing.

Updated For This Edition!

ENHANCED WRITING SECTIONS
are divided into two parts which
provide students with editing and
writing activities to consolidate the
grammar structures learned in
each lesson.

Updated For This Edition!

ONLINE WORKBOOK
powered by MyELT provides students with additional practice of the target grammar and greater flexibility for independent study.

- Engages students and supports classroom materials by providing a variety of interactive grammar activities.

- Tracks course completion through student progress bars, giving learners a sense of personal achievement.

- Supports instructors by maximizing valuable learning time through course management resources, including scheduling and grade reporting tools.

Go to NGL.Cengage.com/MyELT

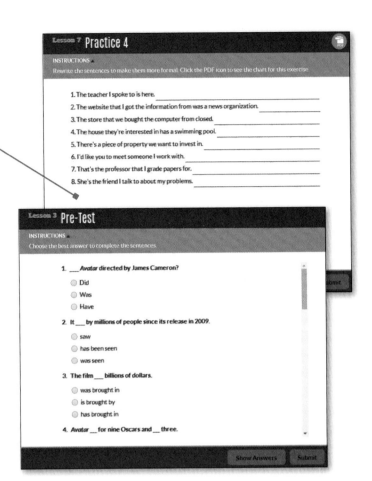

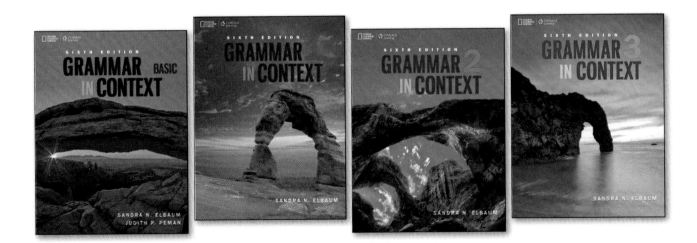

Verb Review

LANGUAGE

Ute petroglyph on Walnut
Knob, east of Blanding, Utah

The limits of my language
means the limits of my world.

— Ludwig Wittgenstein

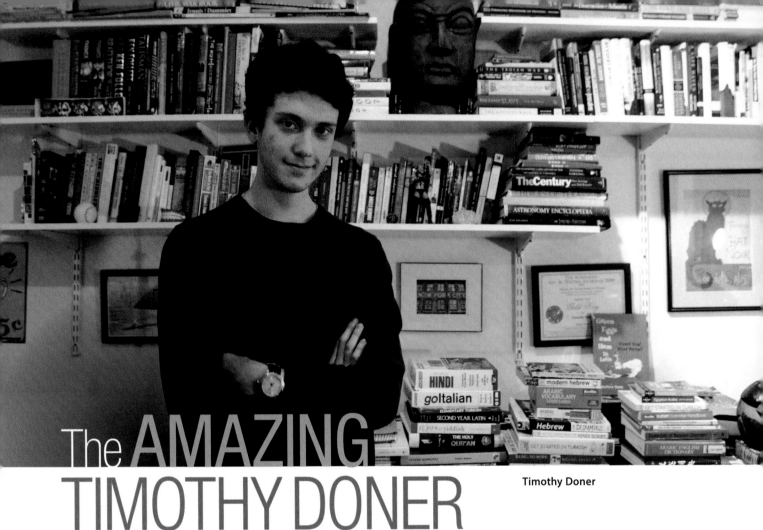

The AMAZING TIMOTHY DONER

Timothy Doner

🎧 **Read the following article. Pay special attention to the words in bold.**

CD 1
TR 2

Timothy Doner **looks** like an average student in his T-shirt and jeans. But there **is** something very special about him. He **speaks** 20 languages. He **doesn't speak** all of them equally well, but he **is** very comfortable in many of them. He **feels** most comfortable with Hebrew,[1] Farsi,[2] French, and Arabic. At any one time, he **is studying** three to four languages.

Videos of him **are going** around the Internet. In one video, he **is riding** in a taxi and **talking** to a Haitian taxi driver in French. **In it, he is telling** the driver that he **wants** to learn Creole, a language of Haiti. In another he **is speaking** Russian with the owners of a video store in New York, where he **lives**. In another, he **is speaking** Farsi with the owner of a bookstore. He **is asking** the Farsi speaker for more information about that language. In other videos, he **is studying** Mandarin or **discussing** the similarities between Hebrew and Arabic with native speakers of these languages. He also **speaks** Urdu,[3] Indonesian, Swahili,[4] and Ojibwe, an American Indian language.

Doner **spends** almost all his time trying to learn languages. To learn some languages, he **takes** classes. To learn others, he **studies** on his own. He always **looks** for opportunities to practice with native speakers. Sometimes he **uses** video chats to practice with native speakers in other countries. He **uses** other methods to improve his language ability: He **memorizes** the lyrics[5] of songs or **watches** movies in other languages. He really **enjoys** himself. He **thinks** that language **helps** you connect to other people. When he **speaks** another language, he **feels like** a different person.

Interestingly, he **doesn't study** Spanish. For him, Spanish **isn't** challenging enough.

---

[1] *Hebrew:* an official language spoken in the State of Israel
[2] *Farsi:* the official language of Iran
[3] *Urdu:* an official language spoken in Pakistan
[4] *Swahili:* a language spoken in Kenya and other countries of the African Great Lakes region
[5] *lyrics:* the words of a song

COMPREHENSION CHECK Based on the reading, tell if the statement is true (**T**) or false (**F**).

1. Timothy Doner always takes classes to learn foreign languages.

2. He prefers to learn challenging languages.

3. It's impossible for him to practice with native speakers in other countries.

1.1 The Present of *Be*

Examples				Explanation
I	**am**			*Be* has three forms in the present: *am, is, are.*
He She It	**is**	from New York.		
You We They	**are**			
I'm surprised about Timothy's abilities. Timothy**'s** an amazing person. He**'s** very intelligent.				Subject pronouns and most singular nouns can contract with a present form of *be.* *I'm, He's, She's, It's, You're, We're, They're, Timothy's*
Timothy **is** smart. Mandarin and Cantonese **are** languages of China. Haiti **is** southeast of Florida. It **is** warm in Haiti all year. I **am** hot. Let's turn on the air-conditioning. Timothy Doner **is** from New York. How old **is** Timothy now? I **am** hungry. What time **is** it in New York now? There **are** many languages in India.				We use a form of *be* with: • a description • a classification • a location • weather • reaction to weather • place of origin • age • physical states • time • *there*
Observe these seven patterns with the verb *be*: Affirmative Statement: Spanish **is** the official language of Colombia. Negative Statement: It **isn't** the language of Brazil. *Yes/No* Question: **Is** Spanish easy for Italians? Short Answer: Yes, it **is**. *Wh-* Question: Why **is** Spanish easy for Italians? Negative *Wh-* Question: Why **isn't** Spanish a challenge for Timothy? Subject Question: What **is** the official language of Brazil?				

Language Note:

We don't make a contraction with *is* if the noun ends in *s, se, ce, ge, ze, sh, ch,* or *x.*

   French is one of Timothy's languages. (NOT: French's)

🎧 **EXERCISE 1** Listen to the first part of a conversation between two students. Fill in the blanks with
CD 1
TR 3
the words you hear.

A: What <u>'s your native language?</u>
                                  1.

B: My native _____ French.
                          2.

A: _____ France?
              3.

B: No. _____ from France. _____ from Cameroon.
              4.   **5.**

A: _____ Cameroon?
              6.

B: _____ in Africa.
          7.

A: What part of Africa _____ ?
                                      8.

B: It's in West Africa.

A: _____ the only language in Cameroon?
              9.

B: No, _____ . _____ many languages in Cameroon, but the two official
              10.   **11.**

languages _____ French and English.
                    12.

EXERCISE 2 Complete the rest of the conversation from Exercise 1 on your own. Use contractions
wherever possible.

A: How many languages _____<u>are there</u>_____ in Cameroon?
                                      1.

B: There _____ about 250 languages. French _____ my official language,
                  2.   **3.**

but my home language _____ Beti.
                                4.

A: _____ similar to French?
              5.

B: No, it _____ . Not at all. They _____ completely different.
              6.   **7.**

A: How many speakers of Beti _____ there?
                                            8.

B: _____ about 2 million.
          9.

A: Then _____ an important language in your country.
                    10.

B: Yes, it definitely _____ .
                              11.

A: My roommate _____ from Nigeria. _____ near Nigeria?
                          12.   **13.**

B: Yes. Cameroon and Nigeria _____ neighbors. Nigeria _____ north of Cameroon.
                                        14.   **15.**

A: I _____ interested in your country, but I _____ hungry.
              16.   **17.**

_____ hungry?
        18.

B: Yes, I _____ . Let's go get something to eat. We can finish our conversation over lunch.
                  19.

1.2 The Simple Present

FORM

Examples	Explanation
I **like** English. You **know** Mandarin. We **come** from China. The people of Iran **speak** Farsi.	We use the base form of the verb with *I, you, we, they*, and plural subjects. Note: *People* is a plural word.
Timothy **lives** in New York. He **studies** languages. Every language **shows** something about the culture. No one in this class **speaks** Ojibwe. Timothy's family **lives** in New York.	We use the –*s* form with *he, she, it*, and singular subjects. We use the –*s* form with subjects beginning with *every* and *no*. Note: *Family* is a singular word.
Timothy **likes to learn** languages.	We can follow the main verb with an infinitive.

Observe these seven patterns with the base form:	
AFFIRMATIVE STATEMENT:	You **speak** Urdu.
NEGATIVE STATEMENT:	You **don't speak** Hindi.
YES/NO QUESTION:	**Do** you **speak** Farsi?
SHORT ANSWER:	Yes, I **do**.
WH- QUESTION:	Where **do** you **speak** Urdu?
NEGATIVE *WH-* QUESTION:	Why **don't** you **speak** Hindi?
SUBJECT QUESTION:	How many people **speak** Hindi?

Observe these seven patterns with the -*s* form:	
AFFIRMATIVE STATEMENT:	Timothy **studies** Farsi.
NEGATIVE STATEMENT:	He **doesn't study** Spanish.
YES/NO QUESTION:	**Does** he **study** French?
SHORT ANSWER:	Yes, he **does**.
WH- QUESTION:	Where **does** he **study** French?
NEGATIVE *WH-* QUESTION:	Why **doesn't** he **study** Spanish?
SUBJECT QUESTION:	Who **studies** Spanish?

Language Notes:

1. *Have* has an irregular –*s* form:

   I **have** a language dictionary. Timothy **has** many language dictionaries.

2. The –*s* form of *go* is *goes*.

   We **go** to college. My sister **goes** to high school.

3. The –*s* form of *do* is *does*. The pronunciation is /dʌs/.

   You **do** your homework at home. She **does** her homework at the library.

4. When we ask questions about *meaning, spelling, cost,* and *take* + time, we use normal question word order.

   What **does** "challenge" **mean**?
   How **do** you **say** "challenge" in your language?
   How **do** you **spell** "challenge"?
   How much **does** a dictionary app **cost**?
   How long **does** it **take** to learn another language?

USE

Examples	Explanation
Timothy **speaks** 20 languages. He **loves** languages, but he **doesn't like** math.	We use the simple present with facts, general truths, habits, and customs.
Timothy **often** practices with native speakers. He **always** tries to learn new things. Does he **ever** use videos? **How often** does he use a dictionary?	We use the simple present with regular activities and repeated actions.

Language Notes:

1. The frequency adverbs are *always, almost always, usually, generally, frequently, sometimes, occasionally, seldom, rarely, hardly ever, almost never, not ever,* and *never.* Frequency adverbs usually come after the verb *be* and before other verbs.

   Timothy is **always** interested in languages.

   He **sometimes** finds native speakers to talk to.

2. We can put *sometimes* at the beginning of the sentence too.

   Sometimes he finds native speakers to talk to.

3. *Seldom, rarely, hardly ever,* and *almost never* have the same meaning. *Seldom* and *rarely* are more formal. Generally, we use *hardly ever* and *almost never* in conversational English and informal writing.

   Do you **ever** speak English with your parents?

   No, I **almost never** do. OR I **hardly ever** do.

EXERCISE 3 Use the underlined verbs to help you complete the sentences.

1. Timothy <u>lives</u> in New York. ___Does he live___ with his parents?

2. He <u>speaks</u> French. He ___doesn't speak___ Spanish.

3. Timothy <u>speaks</u> a lot of languages. _____ Urdu? Yes, he _____ .

4. He <u>memorizes</u> songs. _____ poems too?

5. He _____ video chat. <u>Does he use</u> other methods too? Yes, he _____ .

6. He <u>takes</u> classes. _____ Farsi classes?

7. New York _____ people from all over the world. _____ New York <u>have</u> people

   from Indonesia? Yes it _____ .

8. Some languages _____ accent marks. _____ Hebrew <u>have</u> accent marks?

9. Timothy <u>feels</u> different when he speaks another language. Why _____ different?

10. He<u>'s</u> interested in Creole, but he _____ interested in Spanish. Why _____

    interested in Spanish?

11. Farsi challenges him. Spanish _____ him.

12. He _____ comfortable in Arabic. _____ feel comfortable in Hebrew?

    Yes, he _____.

13. His parents speak English. _____ Hebrew?

14. He is very good at languages. He _____ so good at math.

15. He studies languages every day. _____ from books?

    Yes, he _____.

16. He practices with native speakers. How _____ with native speakers?

17. Not many people speak Ojibwe. How many people in the U.S. _____ Ojibwe?

EXERCISE 4 Fill in the blanks to complete the conversation. Use the words given.

A: Hi. My name's Bai. I'm from China.

B: Hi Bai. My name's Khalid. _Do you speak_ Chinese?
   1. you/speak

A: Well, a lot of people _____ our language is Chinese. But there are several dialects, or
   2. say

   forms, of Chinese. I _____ Mandarin. China _____ over 1 billion people,
      3. speak   **4.** have

   and most people _____ Mandarin, but not everyone does. Mandarin
      5. speak

   _____ over 800 million speakers. What about you?
   6. have

B: I speak Farsi. _____ anything about my language?
      7. you/know

A: No, I _____. Who _____ Farsi?
      8.   **9.** speak

B: People in Iran do. We sometimes _____ the language "Persian."
                           10. call

A: What alphabet _____ ?
      11. you/use

B: We _____ the Arabic alphabet, with some differences. We _____ from
      12.   **13.** write

   right to left. _____ my writing?
   14. you/want/see

A: Yes, I _____ .
      15.

B: تصویر، I want to see your writing too.

A: Here's an example of my writing. 書

B: How many letters _____ ?
      16. Chinese/have

continued

A: Chinese _____ letters. It _____ characters. Each character
           17. not/have   18. have

_____ a word or a syllable.
   19. represent

B: Wow. It _____ like a hard language.
            20. seem

A: Well, it isn't hard to speak it. But it _____ a long time to learn to read and write well.
                                                21. take

B: It _____ so beautiful.
          22. look

A: Your writing _____ beautiful too. And interesting.
                     23. look

EXERCISE 5 About You Tell if the statement is true or false for you. If the statement is not true for you, correct it. Then work with a partner and ask him or her about these statements.

1. I'm from Mexico. F

    A: I'm not from Mexico. I'm from Ecuador. Are you from Mexico?

    B: No, I'm not.

    A: Where are you from?

    B: I'm from the Philippines.

2. I speak English with my friends from my country.

3. I speak English with my family.

4. I want to learn another language (besides English).

5. I am interested in seeing Timothy Doner's videos.

6. My favorite songs are in my language.

7. Most people in my country study English.

8. Spanish is my native language.

9. I'm interested in linguistics.

10. I use video chat to communicate with my friends and family.

11. I know more than two languages.

EXERCISE 6 Read the conversation between two new students. Fill in the blanks by using the words given and context clues.

A: Hi. My name's Marco. I come from Brazil. What _'s_ your name and where __are you from__ ?
                                                      1.   2. you

B: My name's Ly. I'm from Vietnam.

A: How _____ Ly?
             3. spell

B: It's very simple: L-Y. _____ Spanish?
                             4.

A: No. I don't speak Spanish. Spanish _____ the official language of most countries in

5.

South America. But Brazilians _____ Portuguese. What about you?

6.

B: Vietnamese _____ my native language.

7.

A: I _____ anything about Vietnamese. _____ the same

8. not/know   9. Vietnamese/use

alphabet as English?

B: Yes, it _____. But we use many accent marks on our words. Look. Here's a text message I

10.

have in Vietnamese from my sister. Bạn đang ở đâu? _____ all the extra marks we use on

11. you/see

our letters?

A: Yes, I _____. Wow! It _____ very complicated. _____

12.   13. look   14.

similar to Chinese?

B: Not at all. But there's one similarity: both Chinese and Vietnamese are tonal languages.

A: What _____ ?

15. mean/"tonal"

B: It _____ the tone affects the meaning. There _____ six tones in

16. mean   17.

Vietnamese. For example, "ma" _____ six different things, depending on the tone.

18. mean

continued

Terraced rice fields in Vietnam

A: Really?

B: Yes. It can mean "horse," "but," or "ghost." It _____ other meanings too, depending on
19. have

the tone. Tell me about your language.

A: Portuguese _____ some accent marks too. But it _____ tones.
20. have   21. not/have

Not everyone in Brazil _____ Portuguese. There are some other languages too,
22. speak

such as Cocama.

B: How _____?
23. you/spell

A: C-O-C-A-M-A.

B: How many people _____ Cocama?
24. speak

A: I really _____.
25. not/know

B: Right now I really _____ English as quickly as possible. It _____
26. want/learn   27. take

a long time to become fluent in a foreign language.

B: Yes, it does. I have to go now. How _____ "see you later" in Portuguese?
28. say

A: We say "Até mais tarde."

EXERCISE 7 About You Write three questions to ask another student about his or her language.
Then interview this student. (Choose a student who speaks a different language, if possible.)

1. _What is the official language of your country?_____

2. _____

3. _____

4. _____

1.3 The Present Continuous

FORM

Examples	Explanation
We**'re watching** a video of Timothy Doner and a taxi driver. The driver **is telling** him about the Creole language.	To form the present continuous, we use a present form of *be (am, is, are)* + the present participle of the verb (base form + *–ing*).

Observe these seven forms with the present continuous:	
AFFIRMATIVE STATEMENT:	We **are reading** about languages.
NEGATIVE STATEMENT:	We **aren't reading** about animal communication.
YES/NO QUESTION:	**Are** we **reading** about Mandarin now?
SHORT ANSWER:	No, we **aren't**.
WH- QUESTION:	Why **are** we **reading** about languages?
NEGATIVE *WH-* QUESTION:	Why **aren't** we **reading** about Mandarin?
SUBJECT QUESTION:	Who **is reading** about Mandarin?

USE

Examples	Explanation
We **are practicing** English in class now. The teacher **is helping** us learn English grammar.	We use the present continuous for an action that is happening now.
Look at this video of Timothy. He**'s talking** with a taxi driver. They**'re having** a conversation in Creole.	We use the present continuous to describe what we see in a picture or video.
Timothy **is learning** many languages. He **is making** videos of himself. Many people **are becoming** interested in his talent.	We use the present continuous for an action that is ongoing over a longer period of time.
Mandarin **is gaining** popularity as a world language.	We can use the present continuous to describe a trend.
We're from Iran. We **are living** in the U.S. now.	*Live* in the present continuous often shows a temporary situation. It's also possible to say "We **live** in the U.S. now."
Timothy **is sitting** in the back of a taxi. He **is wearing** jeans and a T-shirt.	With certain verbs, we can use the present continuous to describe a state or condition even though there is no action. These verbs are: *sit, stand, lie (recline), wear, sleep.*

EXERCISE 8 Listen to the first part of a conversation between two students. Fill in the blanks with the words you hear.

CD 1
TR 4

A: Look at those people over there. It looks like __they're talking__ with their hands.
1.

Why _____ that?
2.

B: Oh. That's American Sign Language, or ASL.

A: What's that?

B: It's the language of deaf people or people who can't hear well.

A: _____ each word?
3.

B: No. They _____ symbols. Each symbol is a whole word. But sometimes they have to spell
4.

a word, such as a name.

A: How do you know so much about it?

B: I have a nephew who's deaf. _____ to learn ASL because I want to communicate
5.

with him.

A: Where _____ it?
6.

B: At a community college near my house.

EXERCISE 9 Complete the rest of the conversation from Exercise 8 using the present continuous form of one of the verbs from the box below. Use contractions wherever possible.

learn	get	take✓	knit	wear

B: I 'm taking _____ sign language classes with my sister and her husband. Like any new language, it takes
　　　　1.

time and practice. We _____ better every day.
　　　　　　　　　　　2.

A: How old is your nephew?

B: He's three years old.

A: That's pretty young to learn sign language.

B: No, it isn't. He _____ it very quickly, more quickly than we are! Do you want to see a
　　　　　　　　　3.

picture of him?

A: He's so cute. He _____ an adorable hat.
　　　　　　　　4.

B: It's from me. I knit. In fact, I _____ a sweater for him now.
　　　　　　　　　　　　5.

EXERCISE 10 [About You] Tell if the statement is true or false for you. If the statement is not true for you, correct it. Then work with a partner and ask your partner about these statements.

1. I'm forgetting words in my first language. F

　　A: I'm not forgetting words in my first language. Are you forgetting words in your first language?

　　B: No, I'm not. But my younger sister is.

　　A: Why is she forgetting words?

　　B: She's in first grade and all her friends speak English.

2. I'm studying another language (besides English).

3. I'm beginning to mix English with my native language.

4. I'm living with my family.

EXERCISE 11 [About You] Write sentences to tell about something you are learning at this time in your life.

1. I'm learning to budget my time better. _____

2. _____

3. _____

4. _____

1.4 The Present Continuous vs. The Simple Present— Action and Nonaction Verbs

Examples	Explanation
You don't have to speak so loud. I **hear** you. Mandarin now **has** more than 800 million speakers. I **know** something about Farsi.	Some verbs are nonaction verbs. They describe a state, condition, or feeling, not an action. These verbs don't use the present continuous form even when we talk about now. NOT: Mandarin *is now having* more than 800 million speakers.
I **am listening** to a language video. I **hear** some unusual sounds. We **are looking** at a video. We **see** Timothy in a taxi. I'm **thinking about** a major in linguistics. I **think (that)** linguistics is interesting. My mom **is having** a hard time with English. English **has** many irregular verbs in the past. Marco isn't in class today. He **has** a cold.	*Listen* is an action verb. *Hear* is a nonaction verb. *Look* is an action verb. *See* is a nonaction verb. *Think about* or *of* is an action verb. *Think (that)* is a nonaction verb. *Have*, when it means *experience*, is an action verb. *Have* for possession, relationship, or illness is a nonaction verb.
You **are looking** at the video online. You **look** very interested in that video. Timothy Doner **looks like** an average student.	Some verbs can describe either a sense perception or an action: *look, smell, taste, sound, feel.* When these verbs describe a sense perception, an adjective or the word *like* usually follows.

Language Notes:

1. Some common nonaction verbs are:
   - Sense perception verbs: *smell, taste, feel, look, sound, appear*
   - Feelings and desires: *like, dislike, love, hate, hope, want, need, prefer, agree, disagree, care (about), expect, matter*
   - Mental states: *believe, know, hear, see, notice, understand, remember, think (that), suppose, recognize*
   - Others: *mean, cost, spell, weigh*

2. When *see* means *have a relationship with* (personal or professional), it can be an action verb.
   > I'm **seeing** someone new. (I'm dating someone new.)
   > I'm **seeing** an ASL specialist for lessons on signing.

3. Native speakers sometimes use *hope, understand,* and *think* as action verbs.
   > I'm **hoping** to become an English major.
   > If I'm **understanding** you correctly, you're afraid of making a mistake.
   > I'm **thinking** that I need to practice English more. (This use of the present continuous often means *I'm beginning to think . . .*)

EXERCISE 12 Fill in the blanks with the present simple or present continuous to complete the conversation. In some cases, the verb is provided for you. In other cases, use context clues to find the verb.

A: What _____are you looking_____ at?
                    1.

B: I'm looking at a video of Timothy Doner. Listen!

A: What language _____? I _____ it.
                        2.   **3. not/recognize**

_____ it?
4. you/understand

B: Of course. He's speaking my language, Russian! I _____ this for the second time
                                     5. watch

now. I _____ very carefully now and I _____ a few small
         6. listen   **7. hear**

mistakes, but he _____ almost like a native Russian. And he _____ so
                8. sound   **9. know**

much slang. He even _____ like a Russian using Russian gestures.
                   10. look

A: Who _____ to? And what _____ about?
            11. he/talk   **12. they/talk**

B: He _____ to the owners of a Russian video store. They _____
    13.   **14. introduce**

themselves. The Russians _____ surprised to hear an American speak their language so well.
                   15. look

A: Learning so many languages _____ time. I wonder if he has any fun in his life.
                         16. take

B: He _____ languages, and he _____ a great time. Listen.
       17. love   **18. have**

He _____ and _____ with the Russians.
      19. laugh   **20. joke**

A: I _____ that he's amazing. Is he good in other subjects too?
   21. think

B: He says he _____ math.
           22. not/like

A: What _____ to do with so many languages?
         23. he/plan

B: He _____ of becoming a linguist.
       24. think

A: I _____ that's a perfect profession for him.
     25. think

EXERCISE 13 About You Write statements about language and culture.

1. I think that _it's important to be bilingual._____

2. I think that _____

3. I now know that _____

Abamu Degio (left) watches a recording of herself singing a traditional Koro song with Anthony Degio (center) and K. David Harrison (right), who works for the Living Tongues Institute.

The ENDURING[6] VOICES PROJECT

🎧 **Read the following article. Pay special attention to the words in bold.**

CD 1
TR 5

You probably know that there are endangered animals and plants. These are living things that are disappearing. Some animals, like dinosaurs, are already extinct.[7] And many more living things **are going to become** extinct. But do you know that many languages are also disappearing? Every year, several languages go extinct. Today there are more than 7,000 languages. By the year 2100, more than half of these languages **will** probably **disappear**. When the last speaker of a language dies, the world loses the knowledge contained in that language.

Some languages have a lot of speakers. Mandarin, for example, now has 845 million speakers. English has 360 million first-language speakers. The Ojibwe language of Native Americans has about 5,000 speakers. Most of them are older than 65. Other languages have only 1 or 2 speakers. If nothing changes, these languages **will die** when the last speaker dies. The disappearance of languages is happening all over the world.

Why do some languages disappear? Languages like English, Mandarin, Russian, Arabic, Hindi, and Spanish dominate world communication and business. In a part of Russia where the Tofa language exists, parents want their children to learn Russian because it **will permit** greater education and success. Right now there are very few speakers of Tofa. How **will** this language **survive**? **Is** it **going to be** completely lost?

In the project Enduring Voices, linguists visit areas around the world to record native speakers of endangered languages. They are helping many communities preserve their languages online. If you visit the Enduring Voices project online, you **will be able to** hear the sounds of these endangered languages. Even when the last speaker dies, these languages **won't be** lost.

Why are linguists doing this project? Language tells us a lot about a culture. You probably have words in your native language that have no exact translation in English. These special words say something about your culture. When a language dies, an entire culture disappears with it. Seri is a language of Mexico. According to a Seri elder, if one child learns to speak Seri and another child learns to speak Spanish, they **will be** different people.

---

6 *enduring:* long lasting
7 *extinct:* no longer in existence

COMPREHENSION CHECK Based on the reading, tell if the statement is true (**T**) or false (**F**).

1. One language dies each day.

2. Hindi is an important language in business.

3. Technology is helping to preserve dying languages.

1.5 The Future—Form

Examples	Explanation
Many languages **will disappear**. English **will not disappear**. Some languages **won't survive**.	We can use *will* + the base form for the future. The contraction for *will not* is *won't*.
Some living things **are going to become** extinct. The Tofa language **is** probably **going to disappear**.	We can use *be going to* + the base form for the future.
You **are going to hear** some strange sounds if you **visit** the Enduring Voices website. When the last speaker of Tofa **dies**, the language **will die**.	Some future sentences have two clauses: a main clause and an *if* or time clause. We use the future only in the main clause. It doesn't matter which clause comes first.

Observe these seven patterns with *will*:	
AFFIRMATIVE STATEMENT:	Some languages **will disappear**.
NEGATIVE STATEMENT:	My language **won't disappear**.
YES/NO QUESTION:	**Will** English **disappear** soon?
SHORT ANSWER:	No, it **won't**.
WH- QUESTION:	Why **will** some languages **disappear**?
NEGATIVE *WH-* QUESTION:	Why **won't** English **disappear** soon?
SUBJECT QUESTION:	Which languages **will disappear** soon?

Observe these seven patterns with *be going to*:	
AFFIRMATIVE STATEMENT:	We **are going to study** English.
NEGATIVE STATEMENT:	We **aren't going to study** Mandarin.
YES/NO QUESTION:	**Are** we **going to study** French?
SHORT ANSWER:	No, we **aren't**.
WH- QUESTION:	Why **are** we **going to study** English?
NEGATIVE *WH-* QUESTION:	Why **aren't** we **going to study** French?
SUBJECT QUESTION:	Who **is going to study** French?

Language Notes:

1. You can contract pronouns with *will*: *I'll, you'll, he'll, she'll, it'll, we'll, they'll.* In conversation, you also hear contractions with some question words: *who'll, where'll,* etc.

2. In conversational English and informal writing, such as texting, *going to* for future is often pronounced and written "gonna."

🎧 **EXERCISE 14** Listen to the conversation between two students. Fill in the blanks with the words
CD 1
TR 6 you hear.

A: What are you majoring in?

B: I'm majoring in art now, but I <u>'m going to change</u> my major next semester.
                                        1.

A: What _____
                        2.

B: I _____ my master's in applied linguistics.
              3.

A: What's that?

B: It's a degree that _____ me to teach English as a second language. When I
                                    4.
_____ back to my country, I _____ an English teacher.
          5.   **6.**

A: Why do you want to be an English teacher?

A: It _____ easy for me to find a job in China.
              7.

B: Why _____ so easy?
                8.

A: Because everyone there wants to learn English these days.

B: But English isn't your native language.

A: That doesn't matter. I know that if I _____ every day, I _____ fluent soon.
                                                      9.   **10.**

    This semester, I have a Chinese roommate, and we speak Mandarin all the time. But next semester,

    I _____ with an American woman from my math class.
                        11.
    I _____ English with her every day, so my English _____
              12.   **13.**
    quickly. I'm sure of it.

B: You're probably right. You _____ a lot of slang and natural English from her.
                                          14.

A: That's the idea!

B: Do you have any other great plans for your future?

A: After I _____ for a few years, I _____ my own language school
                    15.   **16.**
    in my hometown.

EXERCISE 15 Fill in the blanks with one of the words from the box below. Practice the future with *will*.

| have | teach√ | die | make | be able to hear |
| hear | learn | visit | continue | |

The Enduring Voices project is an important project for several reasons. It ____will teach____

future generations a lot about their past. After all members of a language group _____,
2.

future generations _____ the language of their ancestors. In addition, they
3.

_____ more about the native culture of their ancestors. Also, linguistics students and
4.

professors _____ a record of languages. This project _____ linguistic
5.   6.

research easier. I hope this project _____ for many more years so that we can
7.

preserve information about language and culture. If you _____ the project online, you
8.

_____ languages that are in danger of dying.
9.

EXERCISE 16 Fill in the blanks with the words given. Practice the future with *be going to*.

A: My wife is from Colombia. She speaks Spanish. I'm from Ukraine. I speak Ukrainian and Russian.

B: How do you communicate with your wife?

A: I speak Spanish, so we speak Spanish to each other. But we ____are going to have____ a baby in three
1. have

months. When the baby is born, we _____ to English at home.
2. switch

B: Why _____ that?
3. you/do

A: We live in the U.S. now. The baby _____ the opportunity to speak perfect
4. have

English. We're immigrants, so we _____ in our native countries anymore.
5. not/live

So Spanish, Russian, and Ukrainian _____ so important in our daughter's life.
6. not/be

B: Then she _____ the opportunity to become bilingual or trilingual.
7. lose

A: Well, we think that if we speak three languages in the home, this _____ her.
8. confuse

B: I don't agree. I think it _____ many doors for her in the future. It's so easy for
9. open

small children to learn languages.

A: When she's in high school, she _____ the chance to learn a foreign language.
10. have

B: The best time to learn a foreign language is when you're young. Follow my advice. You won't be sorry.

EXERCISE 17 About You Write about some plans you have for your future.

1. After I finish my degree, *I'm going to return to my country.* _____

2. When I go back to my country, _____

3. After I complete my studies, _____

1.6 Choosing *Will*, *Be Going To*, or Present Continuous for Future

Examples	Explanation
Many languages **will disappear**. Many languages **are going to disappear**. Your daughter **will have** many opportunities if she's bilingual. Your daughter **is going to have** many opportunities if she's bilingual.	For predictions, you can generally use either *will* or *be going to*. *Will* is more common in formal writing.
When the baby is born, we**'re going to switch** to English. I**'m going to start** an English language school in China.	We generally use *be going to* to describe something that was planned before it was mentioned.
I**'m studying** linguistics at the University of Illinois next year.	We sometimes use the present continuous with a future meaning when we have a definite plan. Often, a time or place is mentioned.
A: You should help your kids become bilingual. **B:** Thanks for your advice. I**'ll think** about it. **A:** I'm having trouble with my English assignment. **Will** you **help** me? **B:** Of course I **will**. **A:** I can't hear you. **B:** I**'ll speak** louder. **A:** I'm going to become an ESL teacher. **B:** You**'ll be** good at it.	We use *will* when we make: • a promise • a request for help • an offer to help • a comment of reassurance These sentences do not describe a plan, but the future occurs to the speaker at the time he or she speaks.
My parents **won't support** me if I major in art.	We can use *won't (will not)* to mean *refuse to*.

EXERCISE 18 Choose *will* or *be going to* to fill in the blanks with the verbs given. In some cases, both *will* and *be going to* are possible.

A: Where are you going?

B: To the coffee shop nearby.

A: I 'll go _____ with you. I need a cup of coffee too.
   1. go

B: Well, I'm not really going there for coffee. I _____ a quiet table in the corner and
   2. get

   use the Wi-Fi there. I have to do research for a composition.

A: What topic _____?
   3. you/use

B: I'm interested in animal communication, so I _____ those words and see what
   4. just/google

   I can find.

A: Why _____ about that?
   5. you/write

B: I read an article in *National Geographic* about it. I found it fascinating. So I _____ for
   6. look

   more information about it.

A: I _____ with you anyway. I promise I _____ you. I
   7. go   **8.** not/bother

   _____ a cup of coffee. I have my laptop, so I _____ my e-mail while you
   9. just/get   **10.** check

   do your research.

B: I could use your help a little. I'm not very good with spelling. After I write my first draft,

   _____ me correct the spelling?
   11. you/help

A: Of course, I _____.
   12.

B: I sometimes ask my roommate to help me, but he _____ it. He says I have to do this on
   13. not/do

   my own. This is my first composition for this class, and I'm afraid I _____ a good job.
   14. not/do

A: I'm sure you _____ fine.
   15. do

B: OK, then. Let's go. I _____ the coffee.
   16. buy

A: And I _____ your spellchecker.
   17. be

An UNUSUAL ORPHAN

CD 1
TR 7

Read the following article. Pay special attention to the words in bold.

She **was born** in West Africa in 1965. She **was** an orphan; her mother **died** when she was very small. She **didn't stay** in Africa. She **came** to the United States when she **was** only ten months old. Allen and Beatrix Gardner, an American couple in Nevada, **adopted** her and named her Washoe. **Did** she **learn** to speak English with her new American family? Well, not exactly. Washoe **was** a chimpanzee. And the Gardners **were** language researchers.

The Gardners, who **were** interested in animal communication, **understood** that nonhuman primates[8] can't make human sounds. So they **taught** Washoe American Sign Language (ASL). The Gardners **avoided** using speech around her so that she could learn the way a deaf child learns. Washoe **was** the first nonhuman to acquire a human language.

Washoe **lived** at home with the Gardners. She **liked** to look through books, magazines, and catalogs. She especially **liked** shoe catalogs! Then, when she **was** five years old, language researchers Roger and Deborah Fouts **took** her to the Primate Institute at the University of Oklahoma. There were other chimps there that could communicate with American Sign Language. When Washoe **met** other chimps for the first time, she **didn't like** them. She **called** them "black cats" or "black bugs." Eventually she **started** to interact and "talk" to them.

Researches **wanted** to see if Washoe would communicate with baby chimps using ASL. Washoe **had** two baby chimps, but they **died** when they were very young. Researchers **gave** her a male baby chimp, Loulis, to take care of. Washoe quickly "**adopted**" him. She **started** signing to Loulis. She even **taught** him signs by taking his hands and showing him how to say "food." During her life, Washoe **learned** about 350 signs and **taught** signs to younger chimps.

Washoe **died** in 2007 at the age of 42.

---

[8] *primate:* a member of the highest order of animals, including humans, apes, monkeys, and lemurs

Washoe and Loulis

COMPREHENSION CHECK Based on the reading, tell if the statement is true (**T**) or false (**F**).

1. Studies show that chimps can learn to speak.

2. Washoe taught her own babies how to sign.

3. Washoe spent time with other chimps in Oklahoma.

1.7 The Simple Past

FORM

Examples	Explanation
Washoe **learned** about 350 signs. She **lived** with the Gardners for four years.	Many simple past verbs are regular. To form the simple past of regular verbs, add –ed or –d to the base form. learn → learn**ed** live → liv**ed**
Washoe **had** two baby chimps. She **taught** younger chimps signs.	Many simple past verbs are irregular. have → had teach → taught
Washoe **learned** to sign. She **didn't learn** to speak. **Did** the Gardners **teach** her? Who **taught** her?	We use the past form only in affirmative statements and subject questions. After *did* or *didn't*, we use the base form.
Washoe **was** an orphan. The Gardners **were** language researchers.	The past of *be* is irregular. It has two forms in the past. I, he, she, it → *was* we, you, they → *were*

Observe these seven patterns with a regular verb:

AFFIRMATIVE STATEMENT:	Washoe **learned** American Sign Language.
NEGATIVE STATEMENT:	She **didn't learn** to speak.
YES/NO QUESTION:	**Did** she **learn** 1,000 signs?
SHORT ANSWER:	No, she **didn't**.
WH- QUESTION:	When **did** she **learn** to sign?
NEGATIVE WH- QUESTION:	Why **didn't** she **learn** more than 350 signs?
SUBJECT QUESTION:	How many chimps **learned** to sign?

Observe these seven patterns with an irregular verb:

AFFIRMATIVE STATEMENT:	Researches **taught** Washoe to sign.
NEGATIVE STATEMENT:	They **didn't teach** Washoe to speak.
YES/NO QUESTION:	**Did** they **teach** her American Sign Language?
SHORT ANSWER:	Yes, they **did**.
WH- QUESTION:	Why **did** they **teach** her American Sign Language?
NEGATIVE WH- QUESTION:	Why **didn't** they **teach** her to speak?
SUBJECT QUESTION:	Who **taught** Washoe to sign?

Observe these seven patterns with the verb *be*:

AFFIRMATIVE STATEMENT:	Washoe **was** born in Africa.
NEGATIVE STATEMENT:	She **wasn't** born in the U.S.
YES/NO QUESTION:	**Was** she born in a zoo?
SHORT ANSWER:	No, she **wasn't**.
WH- QUESTION:	Where **was** her mother?
NEGATIVE WH- QUESTION:	Why **wasn't** she with her mother?
SUBJECT QUESTION:	Who **were** her trainers?

For a list of irregular past verbs, see Appendix H.

continued

USE

Examples	Explanation
Washoe **met** other chimps at the Primate Institute. She **liked** to look at books. She **didn't learn** to speak. She **died** in 2007.	We use the simple past to refer to an event that started and ended at a definite time in the past. It can be a single event or a repeated event.

Language Note:

It is not necessary to mention when the action happened, but the simple past implies that a definite time or times can be pinpointed.

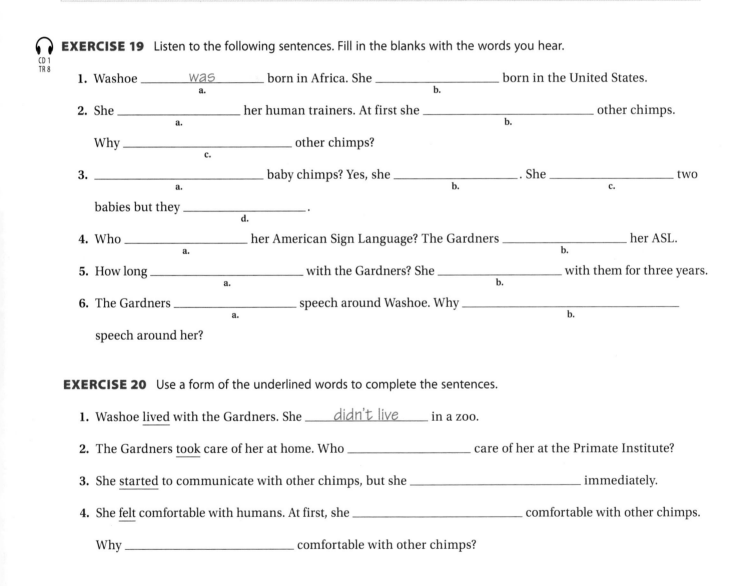

EXERCISE 19 Listen to the following sentences. Fill in the blanks with the words you hear.

1. Washoe _____was_____ born in Africa. She _____ born in the United States.
   a.   b.

2. She _____ her human trainers. At first she _____ other chimps.
   a.   b.

   Why _____ other chimps?
   c.

3. _____ baby chimps? Yes, she _____ . She _____ two
   a.   b.   c.

   babies but they _____ .
   d.

4. Who _____ her American Sign Language? The Gardners _____ her ASL.
   a.   b.

5. How long _____ with the Gardners? She _____ with them for three years.
   a.   b.

6. The Gardners _____ speech around Washoe. Why _____
   a.   b.

   speech around her?

EXERCISE 20 Use a form of the underlined words to complete the sentences.

1. Washoe lived with the Gardners. She _____didn't live_____ in a zoo.

2. The Gardners took care of her at home. Who _____ care of her at the Primate Institute?

3. She started to communicate with other chimps, but she _____ immediately.

4. She felt comfortable with humans. At first, she _____ comfortable with other chimps.

   Why _____ comfortable with other chimps?

5. Researchers <u>gave</u> her a baby chimp—Loulis. Why _____ her a baby chimp?

6. She <u>taught</u> Loulis to make signs. How many signs _____ ?

7. Washoe _____ very old when she died. She <u>was</u> only 42.

8. When _____ ? She <u>died</u> in 2007.

EXERCISE 21 Read the conversation and fill in the blanks with the simple past by using context clues.

A: _____Did you like_____ the story about Washoe?
　　　　　　　1.

B: Yes, I _____ . I liked it very much. Washoe was the first animal to learn human
　　　　　　　　2.

communication. But she _____ the only one. There _____ many more
　　　　　　　　　　　　3.　　　　　　　　　　　　　4.

studies with chimps and gorillas after that. I _____ a program on TV a few years ago
　　　　　　　　　　　　　　　　　　5.

about Koko, a gorilla. Like Washoe, she _____ to make about one thousand signs using
　　　　　　　　　　　　　　　　6.

American Sign Language.

continued

Nim was another chimpanzee who learned to use some American Sign Language signs to communicate.

A: Wow! That's amazing. When _____ 7. ?

B: She didn't die. She's alive and living in California.

A: _____ 8. born in Africa?

B: No, she wasn't. She was born at the San Francisco Zoo.

A: When _____ 9. to train her?

B: They began to train her when she _____ 10. one year old.

A: _____ 11. anything else interesting from the TV program?

B: Yes, I learned a lot of interesting things. For example, when Koko wants something, she asks for it.

One time she _____ 12. a cat and her trainers _____ 13. her a stuffed cat.

But she _____ 14. happy with it. She didn't _____ 15. a stuffed animal. She

wanted a real cat.

A: _____ 16. it to her?

B: Yes, they _____ 17. . They gave her a baby kitten. In fact, she had a choice of kittens and she

_____ 18. a gray male kitten. She even _____ 19. him a name: "All Ball."

A: That's so sweet. So now she has All Ball to play with.

B: Unfortunately, no. One day All Ball _____ 20. away from Koko's cage. He ran into the street,

and a car hit and killed him.

A: Who _____ her about the death of her kitten?
21.

B: Her trainers told her. She _____ very sad. She signed "Bad, bad, bad."
22.

A: What else _____ ?
23.

B: She signed "cry, sad."

A: Did they give her another kitten?

B: Yes. They _____ her two kittens.
24.

A: Wow! What a great story.

EXERCISE 22 About You Find a partner. Tell your partner if the statement is true or false for you. If the statement is false, give the negative form.

1. I knew about language studies with animals. T

   A: I knew about language studies with animals. Did you know about language studies with animals?

   B: Yes, I did.

   A: How did you know about them?

   B: I saw a TV program about this subject a few years ago.

2. I studied English when I was a child.

3. I studied a foreign language in high school.

4. I thought the story about Washoe was interesting.

SUMMARY OF LESSON 1

Compare the uses of the four tenses in this lesson.

We use the simple present:	
With facts, general truths, habits, customs.	Timothy Doner **speaks** many languages. Most Americans and Canadians **speak** English. Mandarin **is** the official language of China.
With a place of origin.	Timothy Doner **is** from New York.
In a time clause or in an *if* clause when talking about the future.	If children **don't practice** their native language, they will forget it. When the last speaker of a language **dies**, the language will die.
With nonaction verbs.	I **think** that animal language studies are interesting. Now I **know** more about animal communication.

We use the present continuous:	
With something that is happening now.	We **are comparing** verb tenses now. We **are reviewing** Lesson 1 now.
To describe what we see in a movie or picture.	Look at that picture of Washoe. She **is making** signs.
With an action that is ongoing over a longer period of time.	Scientists **are studying** animal communication. We **are improving** our English.
With a trend.	People **are using** abbreviations more and more to communicate. Letter writing **is becoming** a less popular means of communication.
With a descriptive state.	Timothy Doner **is wearing** jeans in this video. He **is riding** in a taxi.
With a plan for the future.	We **are finishing** this lesson tomorrow. Next semester, I **am changing** my major.

We use the future:	With *will*	With *be going to*
With predictions.	Some day scientists **will know** a lot more about animal communication.	Some day scientists **are going to know** a lot more about animal communication.
With a request for help or with an offer to help.	**Will** you **help** me with the experiment? Of course, I **will**. I'**ll do** some of the research.	
When a future action occurs to the speaker at the time of speech. There is no previous plan.	A: I forgot my glasses and can't read the story. B: No problem. I'**ll** read it to you.	

We use the simple past:	
With events that occurred once or repeatedly at a definite past time.	Washoe **was** born in Africa. She **learned** about 350 signs. She **died** at the age of 42.

TEST/REVIEW

Fill in the blanks with the correct tense and form of the verb given. Answers may vary.

A: What _are you reading_ ? You _____ *seem* _____ very involved in that article.
           1. you/read   2. seem

B: I am. It _____ a very interesting article about American Indian languages. Many of them
                 3. be

_____ little by little. They _____ extinct. In fact, this article
         4. disappear   5. become

mentions two languages that already _____ extinct more than 50 years ago when the last
                            6. become

speakers _____ .
          7. die

A: _____ that all the members of the tribe are gone?
        8. that/mean

B: No. The tribes aren't extinct. Just the languages. The older people _____ their
                                 9. not/speak

native language with their children when they were small, so the younger generation never

_____ to speak it. When the older members _____ , that was the end of
     10. learn   11. die

the language. Today's tribal members just _____ English.
                          12. speak

A: _____ the voices of the tribe members before they
        13. the Enduring Voices Project/record

_____ ?
     14. die

B: The Enduring Voices Project just _____ a short time ago. So now there _____
                      15. start   16. be

no record of their languages.

A: I wouldn't want my language to disappear. When I _____ kids, I _____
                              17. have   18. speak

my language with them all the time.

B: Me too. If they _____ bilingual, they _____ more opportunities.
                19. be   20. have

A: Some of my friends already have kids. They tell me that their children only _____ to
                                     21. want

speak English. They _____ to speak their language at home anymore.
             22. not/want

B: That's sad. Excuse me but I _____ to continue reading this article now. I have to write a
                 23. need

paper about disappearing languages for my English class.

A: I'd like to know more about the article.

B: Give me your e-mail. I _____ you the link.
         24. send

A: Thanks.

WRITING

PART 1 Editing Advice

1. Use the correct question formation.

   is he
   What ~~he is~~ saying?

   did Washoe die
   When ~~Washoe died~~?

   does "enduring" mean?
   What ~~means "enduring"~~?

2. Don't use the present continuous with nonaction verbs.

   know
   Now you ~~are knowing~~ a lot about communication.

3. Don't use the future after a time word or *if*.

   When I ~~will~~ go back to China, I'm going to be an English teacher.

   I'll learn a lot of slang if I ~~will~~ have an English-speaking roommate next semester.

4. Don't forget *be* when using *going to*.

   are
   We ∧going to study American Sign Language.

5. Don't forget *be* with the present continuous.

   are
   We ∧learning a lot about language.

6. Don't forget *was* or *were* with *born*.

   was   *were*
   Washoe ∧born in Africa.   Where ~~did~~ her babies born?

7. Use the base form after *do, does*, or *did*.

   like
   At first, Washoe didn't ~~liked~~ other chimps.

   Does Timothy ~~speaks~~ French?

8. Use the –*s* form after *he, she, it,* or a singular subject.

   has
   English ~~have~~ a lot of irregular verbs in the past.

9. Use the base form after *to*.

   study
   The Gardners wanted to ~~studied~~ animal communication.

10. Pay special attention to irregular verbs in the past.

    spent
    The Gardners ~~spended~~ a lot of time with Washoe.

PART 2 Editing Practice

Some of the shaded words and phrases have mistakes. Find the mistakes and correct them. If the shaded words are correct, write C.

                were born   C

My parents ~~borned~~ in Poland. Their native language was Yiddish. When they came to the U.S.,
             1.   **2.**

they didn't spoke English at all. They spoke only Yiddish and Polish. I was born in the U.S. When
     3.   **4.**   **5.**

I was a child, I heared mostly Yiddish at home. But when I went to school, I learned English and
          6.   **7.**   **8.**

started to lost my language. Today, very few people speak Yiddish, and I'm thinking the Yiddish
 9.   **10.**

language dying. I only know a few very old people who still speak the language.
      11.   **12.**

    Now that I'm an adult, I feel bad that I didn't tried to speak Yiddish as a child. A few years ago,
                      13.   **14.**

I become interested in Yiddish again. I go to a Yiddish conversation group once a week. One of my
 15.   **16.**

friends asked me, "Why you want to study a dying language? Why you don't study a living language,
                  17.   **18.**

like French or Polish?" She doesn't understands that it's my native language, and this language says
                      19.   **20.**

a lot about my culture. Sometimes, when I speak English, I throw in a Yiddish word like *schlep.* My

friend asks me "What means *schlep*? Why don't you just use the English word?" I answer: There is no
          21.   **22.**

English word that expresses the same thing. Every language have words and expressions that don't
              23.   **24.**

exist in other languages.

    I saw the video of Timothy Doner, and I was surprised that he speak Yiddish. I'm happy that he's
    25.   **26.**

interested in this language too.

    Right now I don't have a lot of time to study the grammar of Yiddish. I only get conversation
                27.

practice. When I will have more time, I going to take a grammar class. I want to keep this language
              28.   **29.**

alive. It's a beautiful, rich language.*

PART 3 Write About It

1. Do you think it's important to keep a record of a dying language? What will it teach future generations?

2. What are the benefits of being bilingual? Give examples from your experience with two languages or the experience of someone you know.

PART 4 Edit Your Writing

Reread the Summary of Lesson 1 and the editing advice. Edit your writing from Part 3.

---

* This is the author's true story.

2

The Present Perfect and the Present Perfect Continuous

RISK

A man stands at the edge of Victoria Falls, in Africa.

Risks must be taken because
the greatest hazard in life is
to risk nothing.

— Leo Buscaglia

The MYSTERY of RISK

Read the following article. Pay special attention to the words in bold.

Have you ever **wondered**[1] why some people take extreme risks? **Have** you ever **thought** about the dangers of exploring an unknown territory? All exploration involves taking big risks. Some explorers **have endured**[2] hunger. Others **have faced** animal attacks or **have survived** extreme weather. Many explorers **have experienced** loneliness, and all **have experienced** uncertainty about the future.

You **have probably heard** of Christopher Columbus. What pushed Columbus to sail[3] across the Atlantic in 1492? And what motivated so many others throughout history to take similar risks?

Some of the reasons behind risk taking are obvious: financial reward, fame, or saving lives. But as the danger increases, the number of people willing to take risks decreases. Only extreme risk takers remain. These are people willing to put their reputation, money, and even their lives in danger. This is the mystery of risk: What makes some people willing to go on when they could lose so much?

In recent years, scientists **have begun** to study the connection between chemicals in the brain and risk taking. They **have found** that the chemical dopamine pushes us to try new things, such as climbing a mountain, starting a company, running for political office, or exploring an unknown territory.

Paul Nicklen, an Arctic explorer, **has been** a photojournalist since 1995. He specializes in photographing polar regions with the goal of teaching people about the wildlife there. In his explorations, he **has come** close to dangerous animals, such as three thousand-pound walruses, in near-freezing water, and **has taken** amazing photographs. Nicklen **has taken** extreme risks to show the world the dangers that animals in these regions face. He **has given** us an extraordinary look at the polar landscape and wildlife and **has received** many awards for his outstanding[4] photography.

Scientists believe that our willingness to take risks to explore our planet **has** always **been** part of the human experience.

---

[1] *to wonder:* to express an interest in knowing
[2] *to endure:* to suffer
[3] *to sail:* to travel by boat
[4] *outstanding:* excellent, extraordinary

Paul Nicklen photographs three Atlantic walruses.

COMPREHENSION CHECK Based on the reading, tell if the statement is true (**T**) or false (**F**).

1. Most people have taken extreme risks.

2. Some people have risked their lives for fame.

3. Scientists have found that a chemical in the brain affects risk taking.

2.1 The Present Perfect — Form

PART A The present perfect is formed with the auxiliary verb *have* or *has* plus the past participle.

Subject	*have/has* (+ *not*)	Past Participle	Complement	Explanation
I	**have**	**taken**	some risks.	Use *have* with the subjects *I, you, we, they,* or *there* + a plural subject.
You	**have not**	**seen**	the photographs.	
We	**have**	**read**	about Nicklen.	
Scientists	**have**	**studied**	brain chemicals.	
There	**have**	**been**	dangers under water.	
Nicklen	**has**	**won**	awards.	Use *has* with the subjects *he, she, it,* or *there* + a singular subject.
He	**has not**	**had**	a serious accident.	
There	**has**	**been**	a study of the brain.	

Language Notes:

1. The contraction for *have not* is *haven't*. The contraction for *has not* is *hasn't*.

   I **haven't** taken a lot of risks in my life.
   Nicklen **hasn't** been to the South Pole.

2. We can contract the subject pronoun with *have* or *has*: *I've, you've, we've, they've, he's, she's, it's.*

   I**'ve** read about Paul Nicklen.
   He**'s** photographed animals under water.

   The apostrophe + *s* can mean *has* or *is*. The verb form following the contraction will tell you what the contraction means.

   He**'s received** an award. = He **has** received an award.
   He**'s receiving** an award. = He **is** receiving an award.

3. We can contract most singular nouns with *has*. We can contract *there* + *has*.

   Nicklen's won many awards.
   This **article's** explained a lot about risks.
   There's been a study of brain chemicals.

continued

PART B Compare statements, *yes/no* questions, short answers, and *wh-* questions.

Statement	Yes/No Question & Short Answer	Wh- Question
You **have taken** a risk.	**Have** you **taken** an extreme risk? No, I **haven't**.	What kind of risks **have** you **taken**?
Nicklen **has swum** in cold water.	**Has** he **swum** in the Arctic? Yes, he **has**.	How many times **has** he **swum** in the Arctic?
Scientists **have studied** the brain.	**Have** they **studied** risk? Yes, they **have**.	Why **have** they **studied** risk?
Nicklen **has taken** underwater pictures.	**Has** he **taken** pictures of sharks? No, he **hasn't**.	Who **has taken** pictures of sharks?

Language Note:

We can add a short question at the end of a statement.

I haven't read the story about Nicklen. Have you?

EXERCISE 1 These are past participles from the reading "The Mystery of Risk." Write the base form and the simple past form of the verb. Then, write if the past participle is the same as (*S*) or different from (*D*) the simple past form.

Base Form	Simple Past Form	Past Participle	Same (S) or Different (D)
wonder	wondered	**wondered**	S
		thought	
		endured	
		been	
		found	
		begun	
		come	
		given	
		survived	

2.2 The Past Participle

Base Form	Simple Past Form	Past Participle	Explanation
work wonder receive	worked wondered received	worked wondered received	The past participle is the same as the simple past form for all regular verbs.
hear leave put	heard left put	heard left put	For some irregular verbs, the past participle is the same as the simple past form.
give take know	gave took knew	given taken known	For other irregular verbs, the simple past form and the past participle are different.

For a list of irregular past participles, see Appendix H.

EXERCISE 2 Fill in the blanks with the present perfect form of one of the verbs from the box.

begin	see	experience	win	take	be	read√	find

1. We _____ *have read* _____ an interesting article about risk.

2. Many risk takers _____ loneliness.

3. Lately scientists _____ to study brain chemicals.

4. They _____ a relationship between brain chemicals and risk.

5. Paul Nicklen _____ a photojournalist for many years.

6. He _____ photographs of wild animals.

7. He _____ many awards for his photographs.

8. I _____ a few of his photographs.

2.3 Placement of Adverbs

Subject	Have / Has	Adverb	Past Participle	Complement
You	have	**probably**	heard of	Christopher Columbus.
I	have	**just**	read	about risk takers.
Scientists	have	**recently**	begun	to study the science of risk.
Scientists	have	**already**	found	that dopamine pushes us to try new things.
Nicklen	has	**even**	come	close to walruses.
His photos	have	**often**	appeared	in magazines.
We	have	**never**	climbed	a mountain.
Nicklen	has	**usually**	had	safe explorations.

Language Notes:

1. Some adverbs can come between the auxiliary (*have/has*) and the past participle.

2. *Already* can also come at the end of the verb phrase. It is more informal to put *already* at the end of the verb phrase.

   He has **already** won a prize. **OR** He has won a prize **already**.

3. *Yet* usually comes at the end of a question or negative statement.

   Have you won a prize for photography **yet**?   No. I haven't won one **yet**.

4. Some adverbs can also come before the subject or at the end of the verb phrase. It is more informal to put the adverb before the subject or at the end of the verb phrase.

   Scientists have **recently** begun to learn about risk. (formal)

   Recently scientists have begun to learn about risk. (informal)

   Scientists have begun to learn about risk **recently**. (informal)

5. Notice the position of *ever* in a question.

   Have you **ever** heard of Paul Nicklen?

🎧 **EXERCISE 3** Listen to the story and fill in the blanks with the missing words.

CD 1
TR 10

I <u>'ve never thought</u> of myself as a risk taker. I _____ to make safe
    1.   **2.**

decisions in my life. I _____ out of an airplane.
                  3.

I _____ a mountain. These things _____ to
        4.   **5.**

me. But then a new friend told me, "I really admire you. You _____ a lot of risks in
                       6.

your life." "No, I _____," I replied. "What _____ that
          7.   **8.**

involves risk?" I _____ that risk meant doing something dangerous. My
          9.

friend answered, "Risk means facing an unknown future. You _____ up your past
                 10.

life to enter a completely different world."

EXERCISE 4 Below is a continuation of the story from Exercise 3. Use the words given to form the
present perfect. Use contractions wherever possible. Add the adverb given.

My friend asked, "How long <u>have you been</u> in this country? Less than a year, right?
          1. you/be

_____ about how many risks you _____ since you left your
    2. you/ever/think   **3. take**

country?"

I started to think about my friend's comments, and I realized that maybe she's right. First, of course,

I _____ learn another language. Even though I studied English in my country, I never had to
  4. have to

communicate with native speakers. My English _____ a lot. But talking
                5. already/improve

with strangers _____ scary for me, especially by telephone.
      6. always/be

I _____ what Americans _____ to me,
    7. not/always/understand   **8. say**

but most people _____ very patient with me.
      9. usually/be

Back home, I lived with my mother. She always cooked for my family and me. But here I _____
                       10. have to

be independent. I _____ to pay bills, rent an apartment, and make my own decisions. I
    11. learn

_____ to cook for myself.
    12. even/learn

In my hometown I walked or took the bus. But here the bus system isn't very good, and almost everyone

drives. So I took driving lessons, got my license, and bought a used car. I used to be afraid of driving, but

little by little I _____ experience and driving _____ easier for me.
    13. gain   **14. get**

Since my friend pointed these things out to me, I realized that I _____ a
                   15. already/make

lot of changes, and each change _____ some risk.
      16. involve

2.4 The Present Perfect — Overview of Uses

Examples	Explanation
Paul Nicklen **has been** a photojournalist since 1995. He **has photographed** underwater animals for a long time.	The action started in the past and **continues** to the present.
Paul Nicklen **has gone** to the Arctic many times. He **has received** many awards for his photographs.	The action **repeats** during a period of time from the past to the present.
Recently scientists **have begun** to study brain chemicals. **Have** you ever **done** anything dangerous?	The action occurred at an **indefinite time** in the past. It still has importance to a present situation or discussion.

EXERCISE 5 Fill in the blanks with the present perfect form of the verb given to complete this paragraph.

Nik Wallenda comes from a long line of risk takers. He doesn't take risks for science or nature. He's a

circus performer; he walks a tightrope. His family, known as the Flying Wallendas, __has been__ in this

 1. be

business for seven generations. Nik started walking on a tightrope when he was two years old. Over time,

he _____ famous for some amazing acts of danger. He _____

 2. become   3. walk

across Niagara Falls and over a deep canyon near the Grand Canyon on a tightrope. So far, he

_____ a serious accident.

 4. never/have

Nik Wallenda walks the tightrope
across the Grand Canyon.

Two climbers on their way to the summit of Mount Everest

Climbing
MOUNT EVEREST

🎧 Read the following article. Pay special attention to the words in bold.

CD 1
TR 11

Have you **ever thought** about taking a risk for the fun or excitement of it? Mount Everest, the tallest mountain in the world, **has always been** a symbol of man's greatest challenge. Located between China and Nepal, Mount Everest **has attracted** mountain climbers from all over the world. In 1953, Edmund Hillary, from New Zealand, and his Nepalese guide, Sherpa Tenzing Norgay, were the first to reach the top. Since then, about 4,000 people **have reached** the summit.[5] But more than 200 climbers **have died** while trying.

Between 1953 and 1963, only 6 people successfully climbed to the top. But things **have changed** a lot in recent years. In 2012 alone, 500 people made it to the top.

What **has changed**? Why **has** the number of climbers **increased** so much **recently**? One reason is that there are more companies leading expeditions.[6] Now 90% of climbers use expedition companies. A climber pays about $100,000 to go up the mountain with a guide. But these guided expeditions **have attracted** a lot of inexperienced climbers. And the

continued

---

[5] *summit:* the top of a mountain
[6] *expedition:* a group journey organized for a specific purpose

crowds[7] **have made** it even more dangerous to make the climb. Danuru Sherpa, who **has lead** 14 expeditions, **has dragged** at least five people off the mountain to save their lives. Some clients don't respect the knowledge and experience of the guides and die as a result.

Has technology **come** to Everest *yet*? Yes, it **has**. As a result, more accurate[8] information about weather conditions at the summit **has made** it easier for expeditions to choose the safest time to make it to the top.

How **has** all of this traffic **affected** Mt. Everest? Lately the mountain **has become** dirty as climbers leave behind garbage and equipment they no longer need. There is now a pollution control committee and lately conditions **have improved** at the Base Camp,[9] but higher on the mountain, the garbage accumulates. One organization, Eco Everest Expedition, **has tried** to clean up the garbage. They started in 2008 and so far they've **collected** over 13 tons of garbage.

According to one climber, Mark Jenkins, "It's not simply about reaching the summit but about showing respect for the mountain and enjoying the journey."

---

[7] *crowd:* a large group of people close together
[8] *accurate:* exact, correct
[9] *base camp:* the main place from which expeditions set out

COMPREHENSION CHECK Based on the reading, tell if the statement is true (**T**) or false (**F**).

1. Most climbers on Mt. Everest have successfully reached the summit.

2. Today, most climbers use a guide.

3. The number of climbers has gone down over the years.

2.5 The Present Perfect with Indefinite Past Time —Overview

We use the present perfect for an action that occurred at an indefinite time in the past. This action still has importance to a present situation or discussion.

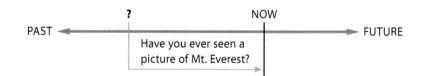

Examples	Explanation
Have you *ever* **taken** a big risk? No, I *never* **have**.	We can use *ever* and *never* to show any time in the past. The time is indefinite.
I've *always* **wanted** to climb a mountain. I've *never* **heard** of Edmund Hillary.	We use *always* and *never* to connect the past to the present.
Has technology **come** to Everest *yet*? Yes, it *already* **has**.	We use *yet* to ask about an expected action. We use *already* with affirmative statements to show that an expected action happened.
Scientists **have** *recently* **begun** to study risk. *Lately* Mt. Everest **has become** dirty. The expedition **has** *just* **reached the top**.	We use *recently, lately,* and *just* with recent past actions.
Everest **has attracted** climbers from all over the world. Over 4,000 people **have** successfully **climbed** Everest.	Some present perfect sentences have no mention of time. The use of the present perfect indicates that the time is indefinite past.

Two climbers ascend this sea cliff in
Maine's Acadia National Park

EXERCISE 6 Fill in the blanks with the words that you hear.

CD 1
TR 12

A: I <u>'ve thought</u> about mountain climbing. I'd love to climb Mt. Everest. It sounds so exciting.
   1.

B: I _____ that it's very dangerous. Many people _____ while trying
        2.   3.

to reach the top. _____ any experience in mountain climbing?
                                        4.

A: No. I _____ a course in rock climbing at my gym.
              5.

B: I _____ interested in risky activities. But I'm happy reading adventure books and
            6.

seeing exciting movies. In fact, I _____ a book about an expedition
                                                          7.

on Mt. Everest. It's called *Into Thin Air*. _____ of it?
                                                                      8.

A: No, I _____ . Is it new?
                9.

B: No. It came out in the 1990s. But it's very exciting. I think you'd like it.

A: Does it have a good ending?

B: I _____ it yet. But I know that a lot of people died on this
                              10.

expedition. Do you want to borrow it when I'm finished?

A: Lately I _____ much time to read because of school. But thanks for the offer.
                    11.

44 Lesson 2

EXERCISE 7 Use the words given to fill in the blanks.

A: I _'ve just seen_ an amazing video of Nik Wallenda. _____ him?
       1. just/see   **2.** you/ever/hear of

B: No, I _____. Who is he?
           3. never

A: He's a tightrope walker. He's from a famous family of circus performers. Take a look at this video online. You can see what he does.

B: Wow! That looks terrific. I'd love to see a circus.

A: There's a circus in town. Do you want to go? I _____ two tickets for
                                              4. already/buy

my girlfriend and me. But I think I can get another one.

B: I'd love to go. I _____ to the circus before. Have you?
                          5. never/be

A: Yes. But not since I was a child. I _____ one recently.
                                  6. not/see

B: What kind of circus is it? Is one of the Wallendas going to be there?

A: No. It's a circus from China.

2.6 The Present Perfect with *Ever* and *Never*

Examples	Explanation
A: Has a climber *ever* **died** on Mt. Everest? **B:** Yes. Many climbers **have died** on Mt. Everest.	We use *ever* to ask a question about any time in the past.
A: Have you *ever* **seen** a movie about Mt. Everest? **B:** No, I never **have**.	We use *never* in a negative answer. For example: No, I never **have**. OR No, he never **has**.
A: Has Nick Wallenda **ever gone** across Niagara Falls on a tightrope? **B:** Yes, he **has**.	We can answer an *ever* question with the present perfect. The present perfect shows no reference to time. The time is indefinite.
A: Has anyone from the Wallenda family **ever had** an accident? **B:** Yes. Nik Wallenda's great-grandfather **fell** to his death in 1978 at the age of 73.	We can answer an *ever* question with the simple past. The simple past shows a definite time (*in 1978, last week, last summer, last Friday, two weeks ago*, etc.).

EXERCISE 8 Fill in the first blank with *Have you ever* and the correct form of the verb given. Then complete the rest of the conversation with the correct form of the verb given and any other words you see.

1. **A:** _Have you ever done_ anything dangerous?

a. do

   B: Yes, I ____have____ .

b.

   A: What was it?

   B: Last year I ____went____ bungee jumping over a canyon.

c. go

   A: Wow! I _'ve never done_____ anything like that in my life. And I never will!

d. never/do

2. **A:** _____ in a helicopter?

a. fly

   B: No, I _____ . Have you?

b. never

   A: No, I _____ . But I'd like to.

c.

3. **A:** _____ a dangerous sport?

a. play

   B: Yes, I _____ .

b.

   A: Oh, really? What sport is that?

   B: When I lived in Spain, I _____ with the bulls. It's very popular in Spain.

c. run

   A: Oh, yes. I think I _____ of that.

d. hear

Bungee jumping

4. A: _____ money in business?
a. risk

B: Yes, I _____ . Ten years ago, I _____ a business.
b.   c. start

A: How did that work out for you?

B: Unfortunately, I _____ a lot of money.
d. lose

5. A: _____ someone from a dangerous situation?
a. save

B: No, I _____ . But my brother _____ .
b.   c.

A: Really? What did he do?

B: A few years ago, he was passing a burning building. He _____ in to save a child.
d. run

6. A: _____ money to a friend?
a. lend

B: No, I haven't. _____ you?
b.

A: Yes. One time I _____ $100 to my best friend.
c. lend

B: Did he pay you back?

A: Yes. He _____ me back two months later.
d. pay

7. A: _____ a mountain?
a. climb

B: No, I _____ . _____ you?
b. never   c.

A: No. But my sister _____ Mt. McKinley last year.
d. climb

B: I _____ Mt. McKinley. Where is it?
e. never/hear of

A: It's in Alaska. It's the highest mountain in North America.

8. A: _____ a big mistake in your life?
a. make

B: Of course, I _____ . I _____ many mistakes in my life.
b.   c. make

9. A: _____ a serious accident?
a. have

B: Yes, unfortunately. Three years ago, I _____ skiing. I _____
b. go   c. fall

and _____ my leg.
d. break

10. A: _____ in a marathon?
a. run

B: Yes. I _____ in the New York marathon five years ago.
b. run

EXERCISE 9 About You Find a partner. Ask each other questions starting with *Have you ever . . . ?* and the past participle of the verb given. If your partner answers *Yes, I have,* ask for more specific information.

1. *swim* across a lake

    A: Have you ever swum across a lake?

    B: Yes, I have.

    A: When did you do it?

    B: I swam across a lake when I was in high school.

2. *go* bungee jumping

3. *win* a contest or a prize

4. *be* in a car accident

5. *fly* in a helicopter

6. *break* a bone

7. *make* a big change in your life

8. *climb* a mountain

9. *lose* money in an investment

10. *risk* your safety to help someone

11. *run* a long distance

12. *play* a dangerous sport

2.7 The Present Perfect with *Yet* and *Already*

Examples	Explanation
Over 4,000 people **have *already* climbed** Mt. Everest. We **have read** about several risk takers *already*.	We use *already* in affirmative statements for an indefinite time in the past. We can put *already* at the end of the verb phrase or between the auxiliary verb and the main verb.
A: I'm planning to climb a mountain next year. **B: Have** you **begun** to train for it *yet*? **A:** Yes, I **have**. But I **haven't trained** at a high altitude *yet*.	We use *yet* or *already* to ask about an expected action.
B: Have you **bought** your equipment *already*? **A:** No, not *yet*.	We use *yet* with a negative verb. We use *not yet* for a short answer.
A: Have you **seen** the new movie *Risking it All* **yet**? **B:** Yes. I **saw** it last week.	If we answer a present perfect question with a definite time, we use the simple past.

Language Note:

1. Using *already* in a question shows a greater expectation that something has happened than using *yet*.

2. We often hear the simple past in questions and negatives with *yet* and in affirmative statements with *already*. There is no difference in meaning between the present perfect and the simple past.

    Have you **bought** the equipment *yet*? = **Did** you **buy** the equipment *yet*?

    No, I **haven't bought** the equipment *yet*. = No, I **didn't buy** the equipment *yet*.

    I **have bought** the equipment *already*. = I **bought** the equipment *already*.

EXERCISE 10 Fill in the blanks to complete each conversation using the correct verb form and *yet* or *already*.

1. **A:** _____ Has _____ your brother come back from his skiing trip _____ yet _____?
        a.   b.

   B: Yes. He _____ came _____ back last week.
                           c.

   A: Did he have a good time?

   B: He _____ hasn't had _____ time to call me _____ yet _____.
                    d.   e.

2. **A:** Is that a good book?

   B: Yes, it is. It's about an expedition in South America. I haven't _____
                                                                                    a.

   it _____. But when I finish it, you can have it.
            b.

   A: Wait a minute. I think I've read it _____.
                                                          c.

3. **A:** I want to see the movie *Trapped on Mt. Everest* this weekend. Have you _____ it
                                                                                              a.

   _____?
            b.

   B: No, not _____.
                         c.

   A: Then let's go. I'm planning to go Friday night.

   B: Sorry. I've _____ _____ other plans for Friday. Maybe we can
                              d.   e.

   make plans for the following week.

4. **A:** What are you going to do during summer vacation?

   B: I haven't _____ about it _____. It's only February. I'll think about it
                           a.   b.

   in April or May. What about you?

   A: I've _____ decided to go to Alaska.
                    c.

   B: You're going to love it. We _____ there a few years ago.
                                                d.

5. **A:** Let's have an adventure this summer.

   B: I _____ told you _____, I'm not interested in an adventure.
                  a.   b.

   A: How do you know? You've never had one.

EXERCISE 11 Circle the correct words to complete this conversation between a grandmother (A) and granddaughter (B). In some cases, both answers are possible. If both answers are correct, circle both.

A: I'm planning to take a vacation next summer.

B: I see you have some information on the kitchen table. Have you (*look*/*looked*) at these brochures yet?
1.

A: No, not (*already*/*yet*). I've been so busy. I (*haven't*/*didn't*) had time (*already*/*yet*). But I've (*already*/*yet*)
2.   3.   4.   5.

decided that I want to have some kind of adventure.

B: Wow, Grandma. These look like exciting trips. How about this one? A kayak trip on the Mississippi River?

A: Oh. (*I've done that one already.*/*I've already done that one.*)
6.

B: I don't remember.

A: (*I've done*/*I did*) it two years ago with my friend Betty.
7.

B: How about skydiving? Have you tried that (*yet*/*already*)?
8.

A: No. I (*never have*/*never had*). But it's not for me. It's a bit too risky.
9.

B: How about this one: white water rafting. It's so much fun. (*Have ever you tried*/*Have you ever tried*) it?
10.

A: No. I (*haven't*/*didn't*). (*Have*/*Did*) you?
11.   12.

B: Yes, I (*did*/*have*). Many times, in fact.
13.

A: It looks dangerous.

B: It really isn't. You wear a life jacket. And the rafting trips are rated according to difficulty. Look.

Here's an easy trip on the Colorado River. (*Have you*/*Did you*) seen this one yet?
14.

A: No, I (*haven't*/*didn't*.) It looks interesting.
15.

B: Should we fill out the application?

A: Wait a minute. I haven't made up my mind (*already*/*yet*).
16.

White water rafting on a river

2.8 The Present Perfect with *Lately*, *Recently*, and *Just*

Examples	Explanation
Lately Mt. Everest **has become** crowded. The number of climbers on Everest **has increased** *recently*. Companies **have** *recently* **begun** to collect garbage on Everest.	*Lately* and *recently* with the present perfect refer to an indefinite time in the near past. We use these words at the beginning or end of the sentence. More formally, *recently* can come between the auxiliary and the main verb.
A: **Have** you **taken** any risks *lately*? B: No, I **haven't**. A: **Has** your brother **done** anything adventurous *lately*? B: Yes. He **took** skydiving lessons last month.	Questions with *lately* and *recently* ask about an indefinite time in the near past. When the answer is *no*, we usually use the present perfect. When the answer is *yes*, we often give a definite time and use the simple past.
I've *just* **come** back from a rafting trip. I *just* **came** back from a rafting trip.	We use *just* for an action that happened close to the present. We can use either the simple past or the present perfect. The present perfect is more formal.

Language Notes:

1. In affirmative statements, *recently* or *lately* with the present perfect refers to something that happened over time (in recent weeks, in recent months, in recent years). With the simple past, *recently* usually refers to a single event.

   Mt. Everest **has had** problems with garbage *recently*. (over a period of time; in recent years)

   My cousin **climbed** Mt. Everest *recently*. (once)

2. *Lately* refers to a repeated or continuous event.

   We **have read** a lot of stories about risk *lately*.

3. Another way to show recent activity is by using *these days*.

   Everest **has become** crowded and dirty *these days*.

EXERCISE 12 Fill in the blanks with the present perfect or the simple past of the verb given.

1. **A:** _____Have you read_____ any good books lately?

      a. you/read

   B: I _____ much time lately. I've been busy with schoolwork. What about you?

      b. not/have

   A: I _____ an exciting book called *The Lost City of Z.*

      c. just/finish

   Lately a lot of people _____ interested in finding this place in South America.

      d. become

2. **A:** I know you love adventure. _____ any exciting trips lately?

      a. you/take

   B: No, I _____. Lately I _____ busy with my job. What about

      b.   **c. be**

   you? _____ anything adventurous these days?

      d. you/do

   A: No, I _____. But my sister _____. Last month she

      e.   **f.**

   _____ rock climbing.

      g. go

continued

3. A: Mt. Everest _____ problems with pollution. Many climbers

  a. have

_____ behind garbage.

  b. leave

  B: _____ recently?

  c. conditions/improve

  A: Yes, they _____. Recently a company _____ to pick up

  d.   e. start

  the garbage left behind by climbers.

4. A: I _____ an article about unusual climbers on Mt. Everest.

  a. just/read

  B: What do you mean?

  A: It's about the first woman, the youngest person, the oldest person, etc.

  B: How old was the oldest person to climb Mt. Everest?

  A: The oldest was 64; the youngest was 16.

5. A: In recent years there _____ a lot of deaths and accidents on Mt. Everest.

  a. be

  B: I wonder why.

  A: Lately a lot of inexperienced climbers _____ to climb the mountain.

  b. try

EXERCISE 13 About You Work with a partner. Ask and answer *yes/no* questions with the words given. If the answer is *yes,* ask for more specific information.

1. go swimming recently

   A: Have you gone swimming recently?
   B: Yes, I have.
   A: When did you go swimming?
   B: I went swimming yesterday.

2. see any exciting movies lately

3. take a vacation recently

4. read any good books recently

5. do anything exciting lately

6. have any adventures lately

EXERCISE 14 Fill in the blanks with the correct form of the words given. Include other words you see.

A: There's a video online about space tourism. _Have you seen it yet_ ?

1. you/see/it/yet

B: Yes, I have. I _____ it a few weeks ago. It was very exciting.

2. see

_____ about going into space?

3. you/ever/dream

A: Yes. I _____ about it lately. Maybe I'll do it someday. It sounds very exciting.

4. think

B: _____ ?

5. you/hear about/the cost/yet

A: No, not _____ .

6.

B: A ticket costs $250,000.

A: I _____ my mind.

7. just/change

2.9 The Present Perfect with No Time Mentioned

Examples	Explanation
I**'ve made** a decision. I'm going to take skydiving lessons. I admire Paul Nicklen. He**'s worked** very hard so we can connect with the polar and marine environments.	We can use the present perfect to talk about the past without any reference to time. The time is not important or not known or imprecise. Using the present perfect, rather than the simple past, shows that the past is relevant to a present situation or discussion.

EXERCISE 15 Fill in the blanks with the present perfect using one of the words from the box. You can use the same verb more than once.

walk	win	give	entertain	photograph✓
be	attract	save	discover	experience

1. Paul Nicklen _has photographed_ marine animals. He _____ awards for his

a.   b.

   photographs. He _____ afraid to take risks. He _____

c. not   d.

   us an amazing look at underwater life.

2. Scientists _____ certain chemicals in the brain that affect risk.

a.

3. Nik Wallenda _____ across the Niagara Falls on a tightrope. He

a.

   _____ people with his performances.

b.

4. Mt. Everest _____ inexperienced climbers lately. One guide, Danuru Sherpa,

a.

   _____ the lives of at least five people.

b.

Sylvia Earle dives to the ocean floor in one of her underwater explorations.

Exploring THE OCEAN

CD 1
TR 13

🎧 Read the following article. Pay special attention to the words in bold.

When she first explored the ocean, Sylvia Earle thought the sea was too large to suffer harm from people. But in just a few decades, many marine animal species **have disappeared** or **become** scarce.[10]

Sylvia Earle is an oceanographer, explorer, author, and lecturer. She **has taken** many risks to explore the ocean. If you put all the time she **has spent** underwater together, it adds up to more than 7,000 hours, or nearly a year of her life. So far, she **has led** over 100 expeditions. In the 1960s, she had to fight to join expeditions. Women weren't welcome. Today she fights to protect marine life.

What **has happened** to the ocean in recent years? Unfortunately, many harmful things **have happened**. For millions of years, sharks, tuna, turtles, whales, and many other large sea animals lived in the Gulf of Mexico without a problem. But by the end of the 20th century, many of these animals were starting to disappear because of overfishing.[11] Drilling[12] for oil and gas on the ocean floor **has** also **harmed** many sea animals.

Earle **has won** many awards for her work. She **has received** 26 honorary degrees from universities and **has been** on hundreds of radio and television shows. In her effort to protect the ocean, she **has lectured** in more than 90 countries and **has written** more than 200 publications. She **has** even **written** several children's books. In 1998, *Time* magazine named Earle its first Hero for the Planet.

Earle said, "As a child, I did not know that people could protect something as big as the ocean or that they could cause harm. But now we know: The ocean is in trouble, and therefore so are we."

She added, "We still have a really good chance to make things better than they are. They won't get better unless we take the action and inspire others to do the same thing. No one is without power. Everybody has the capacity to do something."

---

[10] *scarce:* not plentiful
[11] *to overfish:* fishing so much that the amount of fish available is reduced to very low levels
[12] *to drill:* to open a hole on the earth

COMPREHENSION CHECK Based on the reading, tell if the statement is true (**T**) or false (**F**).

1. Sylvia Earle has been an oceanographer for more than 50 years.

2. Drilling for oil on the ocean floor has harmed animal life.

3. Earle's ideas about the ocean have changed over the years.

2.10 The Present Perfect with Repetition from Past to Present

We use the present perfect to talk about repetition in a time period that includes the present.

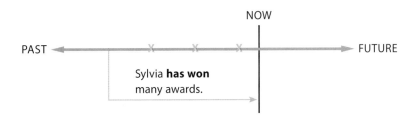

Examples	Explanation
We **have read** several articles about risk this week. Earle **has taken** several risks this year.	When we use *this week, this month, this year,* or *today* to include the present, we use the present perfect. The present perfect shows that the time period is open, and that it is possible for the action to occur again.
Earle **has written** more than 200 publications.	If there is a possibility for a number to increase, we use the present perfect. It's possible that Earle will write more books.
Sylvia Earle **has won** many awards. She **has lectured** in more than 90 countries.	We can use *a lot of, many, several,* or a number to show repetition from past to present.
So far over 4,000 people **have climbed** Mt. Everest. *Up to now*, more than 200 climbers **have died**.	*So far* and *up to now* show repetition from past to present.
How many women **have climbed** Mt. Everest? *How much* time **has** Earle **spent** under water?	To ask a question about repetition, use *how much* or *how many.*
Sylvia Earle **was** the chief scientist of a government organization from 1990 to 1992. Between 1953 and 1963, six people **reached** the top of Mt. Everest.	We use the simple past in a closed time period because the number of repetitions in this time period is final.
Karl Wallenda **performed** on a tightrope many times in his life. He died in 1978. Nik Wallenda **has performed** on a tightrope many times in his life.	If we refer to the experiences of a deceased person (Karl Wallenda), we must use the simple past because nothing more can be added to that person's experience. A living person can repeat an action or experience.

EXERCISE 16 Fill in the blanks with the present perfect using one of the verbs from the box.

| lead | experience | write✓ | disappear | do | go | take | spend | appear | die | reach |

1. Sylvia Earle _____*has written*_____ several children's books.

2. Sylvia Earle _____ many interesting things in her life.

3. She _____ many expeditions.

4. She _____ more than 7,000 hours under water.

5. Many ocean animals _____. They will never come back.

6. Over two hundred Everest climbers _____ .

7. More than four thousand people _____ the top of Mt. Everest.

8. Paul Nicklen _____ under water many times to take photographs of sea animals.

9. His photographs _____ in many magazines.

10. He _____ danger many times.

11. How many photographs _____ he _____ ?

EXERCISE 17 Fill in the blanks with the present perfect or the simple past of the verb given.

1. In 1998, Sylvia Earle _____*won*_____ recognition from *Time* magazine.
   win

2. She _____*has won*_____ many awards in her lifetime.
   win

3. In 2012, she _____ an expedition near Florida.
   lead

4. She's worried that we _____ a lot of sea life.
   lose

5. She _____ many publications.
   write

6. Edmund Hillary _____ the top of Mt. Everest in 1953.
   reach

7. Over four thousand people _____ the top of Mt. Everest so far.
   reach

8. One man, Apa Sherpa, _____ Mt. Everest many times.
   climb

9. Between 1990 and 2012, he _____ Mt. Everest twenty-one times.
   climb

10. Mt. Everest is getting crowded. On one day alone in 2012, 234 climbers _____ the summit.
    reach

11. Karl Wallenda _____ a circus performer. He died in 1978.
    be

12. His great-grandson, Nick Wallenda, _____ many times as a tightrope walker.
    perform

13. In 2012, Nik Wallenda _____ Niagara Falls on a tightrope.
    cross

EXERCISE 18 Fill in the blanks with the present perfect or the simple past of the verb given.

Have you ever heard of James Cameron? You may know him best as a famous movie director.
  1. you/ever/hear

He _____ many movies in his life. Some of his most popular movies are *The*
         2. direct

Terminator, Titanic, and *Avatar.*

But he hasn't always been a filmmaker. When he was a young man, he _____ at several
                                                                    3. work

different jobs. At one time, he _____ a truck driver. But he quit that job and moved to
                                 4. be/even

California to follow his dream—filmmaking.

He _____ many award-winning films. In filming *Titanic* from 1995 to 1997, he
      5. make

_____ make twelve dives down to the ship. At that time, he _____ very
   6. have to   7. become

interested in ocean exploration. He _____ a company, Earthship Productions, in 1998, to
                                     8. form

explore the ocean. Since his first expedition, he _____ at least eight more expeditions.
                                                   9. lead

So far, he _____ the *Titanic* site two times.
           10. visit

Cameron is not only interested in the ocean. He's also interested in space exploration.

He _____ with space scientists and engineers many times.
      11. work

2.11 The Present Perfect with Continuation from Past to Present

Examples	Explanation
Nik Wallenda **has been** a performer *for* many years.	We use *for* to show the duration of time.
Paul Nicklen **has been** interested in sea animals *all his life.*	We can use an expression with *all* (*all his life, all day, all week*) to show duration. We don't use *for* before *all*.
I climbed mountains many years ago, but I **haven't done** it *in* a long time.	In a negative statement, we often use *in* rather than *for*.
Nik **has been** a tightrope performer *since* 1992.	We use *since* to show the starting time.
James Cameron **has been** interested in the ocean *(ever) since* he started work on the movie *Titanic*.	We use *since* or *ever since* to begin a clause that shows the start of a continuous action. The verb in the *since* clause is in the simple past.
I **have** *always* **been** interested in adventure.	*Always* with the present perfect shows the continuation of an action from the past to the present.
How long **has** Sylvia Earle **been** interested in the ocean?	We use *how long* to ask a question about duration.
Paul Nicklen **takes** many photographs during his expeditions. He **has taken** photographs during his expeditions.	Don't confuse the present perfect with the simple present. The simple present refers only to the present time. The present perfect connects the past to the present.

Language Notes:

1. We can use the simple past with *for* when the event started and ended in the past.

    Sylvia Earle **did** research at the University of California from 1969 to 1981. She worked there *for* 12 years.

2. We can use the simple past with *how long* when the event started and ended in the past. Compare

    How long **have** you **lived** in the U.S.? (continues to the present)

    How long **did** you **live** in your country? (completely in the past)

3. We can put *ever since* at the end of the sentence. It means "from the past time mentioned to the present."

    Paul Nicklen became interested in sea animals when he was a child, and he **has been** interested in them *ever since*.

EXERCISE 19 Fill in the blanks with the present perfect and any missing words.

1. Paul Nicklen ___has worked___ as a photojournalist ___since___ 1985.
   a. work   b.

2. The Wallendas _____ circus performers _____
   a. be   b.

   seven generations.

3. Sylvia Earle _____ a good team.
   a. always/have

4. _____ Earle first started to explore the ocean, it _____ a lot.
   a.   b. change

5. In 1953, Edmund Hillary was the first person to reach the top of Mt. Everest. Many people

_____ to reach the top ever _____ .
　　　　　a. try　　　　　　　　　　　　　　　　　　　　**b.**

6. _____ 1990, Apa Sherpa _____ Mt. Everest over 20 times.
　　　　a.　　　　　　　　　　　　　　　　　　　　**b.** climb

7. Ever _____ James Cameron made his first deep sea dive in 1985, he
　　　　　　　　　　a.

_____ many deep sea expeditions.
　　　b. lead

8. How _____　_____ a movie director?
　　　　　　　a.　　　　　　　　　　　**b.** Cameron/be

EXERCISE 20 Fill in the blanks using the correct form of the words given and any missing words. In some cases, no answer is needed in the blank. If that is the case, write Ø.

A: How do you feel about risk?

B: I _'ve been_____ interested in risk taking _____Ø_____ all my life.
　　　　1. be　　　　　　　　　　　　　　　　**2.**

A: So you _____ a lot of articles and books about risk takers.
　　　　　　　3. probably/read

B: Well, yes, I have. But I _____ a lot of risks, too. I _____
　　　　　　　　　　　　4. take　　　　　　　　　　　　　　　　**5.** have

three lessons in parachuting so far.

A: How long have you _____ interested in parachuting?
　　　　　　　　　　　　　　6.

B: Ever _____ I graduated from high school.
　　　　　　7.

continued

A man parachuting smiles as he falls through the air.

A: _____ you ever had an accident?
8.

B: No, I never _____. A few months ago, I read an article about bungee jumping,
9.

and I _____ to do it ever _____.
10. want   **11.**

A: I _____ interested in that. I can't even understand why people would
12. never/be

want to put their lives in danger. In fact, I _____ to do safe things
13. try

_____ all my life.
14.

B: Really? Don't you think that risk is interesting?

A: I didn't say that. Since we _____ to talk about risk in this lesson, I
15. start

_____ more interested. But my interest is in reading about it, not doing it!
16. become

EXERCISE 21 About You Maybe you are already a risk taker and you don't even know it!
Fill in the blanks with the correct past participles to complete the questions. Ask and answer these
questions with a partner.

1. Has your life ____*changed*____ a lot since you left your country?
    change

2. Have you _____ a new career in this country?
    start

3. In this country, have you _____ to do things you've never done before?
    learn

4. Have you _____ something dangerous?
    ever/do

5. Have you _____ to do something no one else has ever done before?
    always/want

6. Have you _____ to make a difficult decision?
    ever/have

EXERCISE 22 About You Work with a partner and talk about:

1. Something you've wanted to do ever since you were a child.

2. Something you've always thought about.

3. An activity you've never tried but would like to.

4. Something you've been good at all your life.

5. Something you haven't done in a long time.

Lonnie Thompson—
ICE INVESTIGATOR

Thompson holds one of the ice samples he has taken from a glacier.

Read the following article. Pay special attention to the words in bold.

Lonnie Thompson **has been climbing** to the top of glaciers[13] for over 40 years. He **has been looking** for information that is hidden inside the ice. Some of these glaciers contain information that is thousands of years old. This information shows that the planet **has been warming** and the ice of these glaciers **has been melting**. He wants to find out more about these glaciers before it's too late.

Thompson has probably spent more time above 18,000 feet than anyone else. Altogether he has spent over 1,100 days at this altitude. Many people have climbed to above 18,000 feet, but no one has stayed there as long as Thompson. Sometimes he has stayed at this altitude for up to six consecutive[14] weeks.

He has faced many dangers and challenges. Getting six tons of camping and drilling equipment up to 23,500 feet is one. Lightning is another. "I've had lightning come down ten feet in front of me," he reported. Other dangers are avalanches,[15] storms, and wind. What's amazing is that Thompson is in his 60s. At the age of 63, he had a heart transplant. His father died at 41 of a heart attack. "Maybe I'm living longer because I climb mountains," he said.

Thompson has gone to a glacier in Peru twenty-six times. Because of his research, we **have been learning** more about the past. But the opportunities for gaining this knowledge **have been diminishing**.[16] "It's like visiting a patient dying of cancer. You know there's no hope; you can only watch it shrink away. So my work has become a way to capture[17] history before it disappears forever."

---

[13] *glacier:* a large mass of ice that moves slowly, usually down a mountain
[14] *consecutive:* following one after the other in regular order
[15] *avalanche:* a sudden break of snow down a mountain
[16] *to diminish:* to decrease in number, to lessen
[17] *to capture:* to catch

COMPREHENSION CHECK   Based on the reading, tell if the statement is true (**T**) or false (**F**).

1. Lonnie Thompson has been finding important information in glaciers.

2. He has been climbing glaciers for twenty-six years.

3. Some of the glaciers have been melting.

2.12 The Present Perfect Continuous

The present perfect continuous is formed with the auxiliary verb *have/has* + *been* + the present participle (verb *-ing*).

```
                              NOW
PAST ◄─────────────────────────┬──────────────────► FUTURE
          │                     │
          │  He has been taking risks
          │  since he was a small child.
          └─────────────────────┘
```

Examples	Explanation
Lonnie Thompson **has been climbing** glaciers *for* many years. Paul Nicklen **has been taking** risks *since* he was a small child.	We use the present perfect continuous to talk about an action that started in the past and continues to the present. We use *for* and *since* or *ever since* to show the time spent at an activity.
Lately people **have been thinking** about space tourism.	An indefinite time word, like *lately*, can be used.
We **have been reading** stories about risk takers.	Sometimes there is no mention of time.
He **has worked** with glaciers for a long time. He **has been working** with glaciers for a long time.	With some verbs, we can use either the present perfect or the present perfect continuous with no difference in meaning. This is especially true with the following verbs: *live, work, teach, study, use, wear*.
How long has James Cameron **been making** movies? *How long* has Lonnie Thompson **been studying** glaciers?	To ask a question about the duration of an action, we use *how long*.
Thompson **studies** glaciers. He **has been studying** glaciers for over 40 years. Many glaciers **are melting**. They **have been melting** for many years.	Don't confuse the simple present or the present continuous with the present perfect continuous. The present perfect continuous connects the past to the present.

Observe these seven patterns with the present perfect continuous:

AFFIRMATIVE STATEMENT:	Thompson **has been studying** glaciers.
NEGATIVE STATEMENT:	He **hasn't been studying** the ocean.
YES/NO QUESTION:	**Has** he **been studying** glaciers in Peru?
SHORT ANSWER:	Yes, he **has**.
WH- QUESTION:	Which glaciers **has** Thompson **been studying**?
NEGATIVE WH- QUESTION:	Why **hasn't** he **been studying** the ocean?
SUBJECT QUESTION:	Who **has been studying** the ocean?

EXERCISE 23 Fill in the blanks with the present perfect continuous form of the verb given. Add *for* or *since* where necessary.

1. James Cameron <u>has been making</u> movies <u>since</u> 1984.
   make

2. He _____ the ocean _____ many years.
   explore

3. Lately he _____ with space scientists.
   work

4. Lonnie Thompson _____ glaciers _____ over 40 years.
   study

5. He _____ a lot about the past.
   learn

6. _____ many years, the glaciers _____ .
   melt

7. The Wallenda family _____ risky activities _____ seven generations.
   perform

8. Scientists _____ more and more about how brain chemicals affect risk.
   learn

9. Sylvia Earle _____ the ocean _____ many years.
   study

10. People _____ Mt. Everest _____ 1953.
    climb

EXERCISE 24 Fill in the blanks in the following conversations. Use the simple present or the present perfect continuous. Fill in any other missing words.

1. **A:** I'm learning about glaciers.

   B: How long <u>have you been learning</u> about glaciers?
   a.

   A: <u>For</u> about six months.
   b.

2. **A:** My father works as a photographer.

   B: How long _____ as a photographer?
   a.

   A: _____ about 10 years.
   b.

3. **A:** Are you thinking about getting your pilot's license?

   B: Yes, I am.

   A: How long _____ about getting it?
   a.

   B: _____ I was in high school.
   b.

continued

4. A: Someone told me that your mother is a mountain climber.

   B: That's right. She is.

   A: How _____ mountains?

a.

   B: _____ about 20 years.

b.

5. A: James Cameron makes great movies.

   B: I agree. How _____ movies?

a.

   A: He's _____ making movies _____ over 35 years. And he's been

b.   c.

   _____ risks to make some of these movies.

d.

   B: Do you mean that he's put his life in danger?

   A: Sometimes. But he _____ taking financial risks too.

e.

6. A: You've _____ reading that book for a long time.

a.

   B: Yes, I _____. It's so interesting. It's called *Into Thin Air*.

b.

   A: I've never heard of it.

   B: Yes, you have. I _____ you about it _____ a few weeks.

c.   d.

   A: Tell me again.

   B: It's about a tragedy on Mt. Everest.

7. A: I _____ an interesting book by Sylvia Earle.

a.

   B: Can you read a science book? I can't.

   A: It's a children's book. So it's easy to understand.

EXERCISE 25 `About You` Work with a partner and talk about:

1. Something you've been thinking about since we started this lesson.

2. Something you've been learning or studying for many years.

3. Something that has been changing in your life.

2.13 The Present Perfect, the Present Perfect Continuous, and the Simple Past

Examples	Explanation
Lonnie Thompson **has been trying** to find information in glaciers. How long **has** Paul Nicklen **been working** as a photojournalist?	We use the present perfect continuous for actions that started in the past and are still happening now. These actions are ongoing and are not finished. For questions about duration, we use *how long*.
Thompson **has climbed** many glaciers. **Have** you **ever** climbed a mountain? I **have** always **wanted** to climb a mountain, but I **have** never **done** it. Lonnie Thompson **has been** interested in glaciers for many years. How many times **has** Thompson **gone** to Peru? How much time **has** he **spent** on glaciers?	We use the present perfect, not the present perfect continuous, in the following cases: • with repetition from past to present • with an indefinite time in the past • with *always* and *never* • for duration with nonaction* verbs • with questions about repetition, using *how much* or *how many*
Compare: (a) I**'ve read** some interesting articles lately. (b) I **have been reading** a book about glaciers. (a) I **have climbed** several mountains since 2010. (b) My friend **has been climbing** a mountain in Alaska for the last three days.	Sentences (a) indicate an indefinite past time. Sentences (b) indicate that the activity is still in progress.
He **has worked** as a photographer for many years. He **has been working** as a photographer for many years.	In some cases, there is no difference in meaning between the present perfect and the present perfect continuous.
When he was in college, Lonnie Thompson **studied** geology. He **made** his first glacier exploration in the 1970s.	We use the simple past for an action that was completely in the past. Often a definite time is mentioned.

*For a list of nonaction verbs, see page 16.

EXERCISE 26 Listen to the story of Jill Seaman. Fill in the blanks with the missing words.

CD 1
TR 15

Jill Seaman _____is_____ an American doctor. She _____ as a

                 1.   2.

doctor _____ 1979. She _____ ways to bring modern

            3.   4.

medicine to South Sudan _____ many years. When she _____ in Sudan in

                               5.   6.

1989, many people in this region were very sick. At the same time, a war was going on. She _____

                                                                                                      7.

to South Sudan with an organization called Doctors Without Borders. Doctors from this organization

_____ to countries all over the world to help where there is a need for

            8.

continued

medical care. When Seaman first _____ to South Sudan, there _____ no
9.   10.

doctors treating patients in small villages. Over the past twenty years, the health of the people in South

Sudan _____. In one year alone, Doctors Without Borders
11.

_____ two thousand five hundred people.
12.

    Because of the war, Seaman _____ many terrible things. But she says she's not a
13.

risk taker. She says, "Everybody _____ risks. Life _____ a risk." But
14.   15.

_____ many years, she _____ thousands of people.
16.   17.

"How could I be more lucky?" she says.

EXERCISE 27 Fill in the blanks with the present perfect, the present perfect continuous, or the
simple past of the verb given.

    Alex Honnold is a mountain climber. He _has been climbing_ since he was a child. What's amazing
                                                             1. climb

is that he _____ this many times without a rope or any protection. This kind of
2. do

climbing is called "free soloing." He _____ more than a thousand free-solo climbs.
3. make

When he was a small child, he _____ by practicing at a gym in Sacramento,
4. begin

California, where he lived. He _____ there six days a week. Throughout his life,
5. go

he _____ his risk. In 2008, to prepare for a climb in Yosemite National
6. increase

Park, he _____ ropes. He wanted to analyze the mountain. He was looking for the
7. use

best places for his hands and feet. The next day, he _____ it to the top without
8. make

ropes. And he _____ it in less than 3 hours.
9. do

    He _____ on many TV shows and in many magazines. In 2011 he
10. appear

_____ on the cover of *National Geographic* magazine.
11. be

Alex Honnold dangles from an overhang as he climbs a rock mountain in Oman.

EXERCISE 28 Fill in the blanks with the present perfect or the present perfect continuous. Use context clues to help you. In some cases, more than one answer is possible.

1. Alex is climbing a mountain now. He <u>has been climbing</u> that mountain for eight hours.

   He _____ that mountain five times.

2. Alex is preparing for his next climb. He _____ for several months.

3. I like to see adventure movies. I _____ many James Cameron movies.

   _____ you ever _____ a James Cameron movie?

4. I _____ a few risks in my life. For example, I took a risk when I left my country and

   went to live in another country.

5. Jill Seaman _____ people in poor countries. Because of her help, conditions have

   been improving for these people.

6. Sylvia Earle _____ as a National Geographic explorer since 1998. She loves her work.

7. Let's move on to a new subject. I don't want to talk about risk anymore. We _____

   about it for three days!

SUMMARY OF LESSON 2

Compare the simple present and the present perfect.

Simple Present	Present Perfect
Paul Nicklen **is** a photojournalist.	He **has been** a photojournalist since 1985.

Compare the present continuous and the present perfect continuous.

Present Continuous	Present Perfect Continuous
Jill Seaman **is helping** people in Africa.	She **has been helping** people in Africa for many years.

Compare the simple past and the present perfect.

Simple Past	Present Perfect
James Cameron **made** 12 deep-sea dives between 1995 and 1997.	James Cameron **has made** many dives since 1995.
When **did** Sylvia Earle **start** her career?	How long **has** she **had** her career?
Did Thompson **find** something important last year?	**Has** Thompson ever **gone** to the South Pole?
Nik Wallenda's grandfather **had** an accident and **died**.	Nik Wallenda takes risks, but he **has** always **been** very careful.

Compare the present perfect and the present perfect continuous with no difference in meaning.

Present Perfect	Present Perfect Continuous
Thompson **has studied** glaciers for many years.	Thompson **has been studying** glaciers for many years.

Compare the present perfect and the present perfect continuous with a difference in meaning.

Present Perfect	Present Perfect Continuous
I need a new hobby. I **have thought** about mountain climbing.	Lately, I **have been thinking** a lot about my future.
He **has climbed** the mountain three times.	He **has been climbing** the mountain for three hours.

TEST/REVIEW

Fill in the blanks with the simple past, the present perfect, or the present perfect continuous of the verb given. Fill in any other missing words. In some cases, more than one answer is possible.

A: I ___*haven't seen*___ you _____ a long time. Where _____ for
      1. not/see   2.   3. be
the past few months?

B: Lately I _____ a lot of work. And I have a new hobby. So I _____
              4. have   5. not/have
a lot of time for social activities lately.

A: What's your new hobby?

B: I _____ skydiving lessons lately.
              6. take

A: You are? Really? That sounds so interesting—and scary! How long _____ that?
                                                                        7. you/do

B: I _____ to take lessons about six months ago. So far, I _____ out
              8. start   9. jump
of airplanes about 10 or 12 times.

A: You're so brave. I can't imagine doing that. In fact, I _____ about it.
                                                              10. never/even/think

B: I _____ to do it, ever _____ I was a little girl. Before I started, I
              11. always/want   12.
_____ to some experienced jumpers. I _____ to learn a lot before doing it.
      13. talk   14. have

A: _____ a scary experience?
        15. you/ever/have

B: No. I'm very careful.

A: I'm glad to hear that. Is this an expensive hobby?

B: Yes. It's very expensive. I _____ to buy a lot of equipment over the past six
                                      16. have
months. And each jumps costs me $150.

A: Wow! That's a lot of money.

B: That's why I _____ overtime a lot lately. _____ the past
                    17. work   18.
few months, I _____ to convince my husband to do it with me, but he's not
                  19. try
interested at all. What about you? What kind of hobbies do you have?

A: I'm not as brave as you are. My hobby is a very safe one. I knit. My grandmother _____ me
                                                                                        20. teach
how to knit when I _____ ten years old, and I _____ ever
                    21. be   22. knit
_____ . I _____ hundreds of scarves and sweaters over the years.
      23.   24. make

B: Would you like to try skydiving with me sometime?

A: No, thanks! Would you like to learn to knit?

B: No, thanks.

WRITING

PART 1 Editing Advice

1. Don't confuse the present participle (verb–*ing*) and the past participle. In some cases, they sound similar.

    > taken
    > Paul Nicklen has ~~taking~~ many pictures.
    > been
    > Has he ever ~~being~~ to the South Pole?

2. Don't confuse *for* and *since*.

    > for
    > Sylvia Earle has been studying the ocean ~~since~~ many years.

3. Use the correct word order.

    > never been
    > I have ~~been never~~ to Niagara Falls.
    > ever had
    > Has Wallenda ~~had ever~~ an accident?

4. Use *yet* in negative statements. Use *already* in affirmative statements.

    > yet
    > He hasn't reached the top of the mountain ~~already~~.

5. Don't forget the *-d* or *-ed* ending on past participles of regular verbs.

    > ed
    > We have learn_ many things about risk takers.
    > d
    > I've decide_ to take sky-diving lessons.

6. Use correct subject-verb agreement.

    > have
    > Some people ~~has~~ had very interesting experiences.

PART 2 Editing Practice

Some of the shaded words and phrases have mistakes. Find the mistakes and correct them. If the shaded words are correct, write *C*.

My uncle Meyer is not a famous person. But he has <u>doing</u> [done] many great things in his life. He is a
                                                       1.
teacher. He <u>has been teaching</u> Hebrew and Jewish history <u>since</u> [for] the past 45 years. He <u>has inspire</u> [d]
            2.   **3.**   **4.**
many young people to love language and history. In some cases, he <u>have</u> [has] taught three generations
                                                                   5.
of the same family. He often <u>receives</u> [C] letters and e-mails from students who <u>have studied</u> [studied] with him
                             6.   **7.**
many years ago. Many of them <u>has</u> [have] finished college and started their own careers and families. They
                             8.
often tell him how much they learned from him and how much he <u>has</u> [C] inspired them.
                                                               9.

Another great thing about my uncle is that he has always being a great teacher outside the
10.
classroom. When we have been children, he often took us to the library on Saturdays and to a
11.   12.
museum on Sundays. He has been always a member of several museums and has donated money to
13.   14.
support them. Many times we have wondered why it's important to support the museums. He once
15.
has told us, "The classroom is only one place to learn. But life is bigger than the classroom. There are
16.

many other ways to learn."

A third great thing about Uncle Meyer is that he never stops learning. He's 68 years old now, and
he has recently decided to learn Chinese. He has already learn Russian and German pretty well and
17.   18.   19.
now he wants a new challenge. He is studying Chinese for the past two months. He speaks it a little
20.   21.   22.
now, but he hasn't learned to read or write it yet. But he never gives up. He has always wanted to
23.   24.   25.
travel to China and now he's hoping to go there next year with the ability to speak some Chinese.

Some people think he's old and he should retire. But he has never been thinking about retiring.
26.

He loves to teach and learn. He has taught me that it's important to learn and inspire other people
27.

to learn.

PART 3 Write About It

1. Choose a living person you know or have read about that has done great things. This person
doesn't have to be famous or well known. Write a paragraph (or multiple paragraphs) describing
what this person has done and why you think he or she is great. Has this person taken a big risk?
Has this person made an important discovery? Has this person inspired other people?

2. Sometimes we take a big risk or make a decision to do something new without thinking
through the consequences. Write a paragraph (or multiple paragraphs) telling about a decision
you made or a risk you took without thinking things through. What was the decision? How has
this decision affected your life or the lives of those around you? What have you learned from
this experience?

PART 4 Edit Your Writing

Reread the Summary of Lesson 2 and the editing advice. Edit your writing from Part 3.

Passive and Active Voice

An outdoor movie plays in front of the Brooklyn Bridge.

THE
MOVIES

Every great film should
seem new every time
you see it.

— Roger Ebert

OSCAR NIGHT IN HOLLYWOOD

Angelina Jolie and Brad Pitt at the 2014 Academy Awards, in Hollywood, California.

🎧 **Read the following article. Pay special attention to the words in bold.**

CD 1
TR 16

The movie stars are arriving to walk the red carpet to the Dolby Theater. As they are getting out of their limousines,[1] they **are being photographed** from every angle. The women **are being interviewed** about their choice of gowns,[2] and they **are** always **told** how beautiful they look. People at home are starting to gather around their TVs to see their favorite stars. It's Oscar night in Hollywood. The Dolby Theater will fill up with more than three thousand people from the movie industry and their guests.

If you have seen this show, you know that these awards (also known as the Academy Awards) **are given** out each year in February or March. A few months before the show, the nominees[3] **are announced**. Movie critics[4] often make predictions about who will win in each category.

The awards **are presented** in twenty-four categories: best foreign film, best actor, best music, and best costume, to name a few. But the audience **is** not **given** the results quickly. In fact, the show often lasts more than two hours, with suspense[5] building until the last winner **is announced**—the Best Picture of the year.

This is how it **is done** today. But when the awards ceremony started in 1929, only fifteen awards **were presented** and the ceremony **was attended** by only 250 people. Tickets cost $10 (about $139 in today's dollars), and anyone who could afford a ticket could attend. Until 1941, the winners' names **were** already **known** before the ceremony and **published** in newspapers the night before. So there was not much suspense. But when television **was invented** and came into more and more people's homes, Oscar night started to become the spectacular show that it is today. Since 1953, Oscar night **has been televised** and **broadcast**[6] all over the world. This show **is seen** by millions of people.

---

1 *limousine:* a large, expensive car, usually with a driver
2 *gown:* a long, formal dress for women
3 *nominee:* a person recommended to receive an award
4 *movie critic:* a person who reviews and gives opinions about movies
5 *suspense:* a feeling of anxiety and tension about a future event
6 *to broadcast:* to send over the radio or the TV

COMPREHENSION CHECK Based on the reading, tell if the statement is true (**T**) or false (**F**).

1. Both the actors and the actresses are asked about their choice of clothes.

2. The number of Oscars presented has always been the same.

3. At one time, an invitation was not needed to attend the Oscar presentation.

3.1 Active and Passive Voice — Introduction

Examples	Explanation
subject verb object **Active:** The children **saw** the movie. subject verb agent **Passive:** The movie **was seen** *by* the children.	Some sentences are in the **active voice**. The subject performs the action of the verb. Some sentences are in the **passive voice**. The subject receives the action of the verb. The passive voice is formed with *be* + the past participle.
The dress **was designed** by Prada. The next award **will be presented** by Brad Pitt. The actresses **are photographed** from every angle. The awards **are presented** in 24 categories.	Sometimes the agent is used. If so, the agent follows *by*. More often, the agent is omitted.
Active: He photographed **her**. **Passive: She** was photographed by **him**.	Notice the difference in pronouns in an active sentence and a passive sentence. After *by*, the object pronoun is used.
In 1929, tickets **were** sold for $10. (simple past) Today tickets **are** not **sold**. (simple present)	The tense of the passive sentence is shown with the verb *be*. The past participle is used with every tense.

Language Notes:

1. If two verbs in the passive voice are connected with *and*, we do not repeat the verb *be*.

    The Oscar ceremony **is televised and seen** by millions of people.

2. An adverb can be placed between *be* and the main verb.

    Before 1941, the winners' names **were** *already* **known** before the ceremony.
    Today the winners **are** *never* **announced** ahead of time.

Compare these patterns with the passive voice in the past.

AFFIRMATIVE STATEMENT:	The movie **was filmed** in the United States.
NEGATIVE STATEMENT:	It **wasn't filmed** in Canada.
YES/NO QUESTION:	**Was** it **filmed** in Hollywood?
SHORT ANSWER:	No, it **wasn't**.
WH- QUESTION:	When **was** it **filmed**?
NEGATIVE *WH-* QUESTION:	Why **wasn't** it **filmed** in Hollywood?
SUBJECT QUESTION:	Which movie **was filmed** in Canada?

3.2 Comparison of Active and Passive Voice

Compare active and passive voice with different tenses and with modals.

	Active	Passive
Simple Present	A committee **chooses** the winners.	The winners **are chosen** weeks before.
Present Continuous	Brad Pitt **is presenting** an award now.	The award **is being presented** for the best movie.
Future	An actress **will announce** the winner's name. An actress **is going to announce** the winner's name.	The winner's name **will be announced** in a few minutes. The winner's name is **going to be announced** in a few minutes.
Simple Past	The director **made** a new movie.	The movie **was made** in Paris.
Past Continuous	Reporters **were interviewing** the stars.	The stars **were being interviewed** on the red carpet.
Present Perfect	Woody Allen **has made** many movies.	Most of his movies **have been made** in New York.
Modal	You **should see** the movie in the theater.	The movie **should be seen** on a large screen.

EXERCISE 1 Listen to the following sentences and fill in the blanks with the words you hear. Then decide if the verb is active (A) or passive (P).

CD 1
TR 17

1. Angelina Jolie _____ presented _____ an Oscar. A

2. Angelina Jolie _____ was presented _____ an Oscar. P

3. The actress _____ a beautiful dress.

4. The dress _____ specially for her.

5. Who _____ the dress?

6. The actress _____ and _____ .

7. Many American actors _____ in California.

8. _____ all American movies _____ in Hollywood?

9. The movie _____ in 3-D.

10. When the winners _____ the award, they _____

a "thank you" speech.

11. In 1929, only one Oscar _____ to a woman.

12. Some films _____ in New York.

13. _____ you ever _____ *Gone With the Wind*?

14. When _____ this film _____?

15. Some movies _____ on TV.

16. The theater near my house was closed because it _____ .

17. Which movie _____ in Paris?

18. I _____ to the movies lately.

EXERCISE 2 This is a conversation about movies. Fill in the blanks with the passive voice of the verb given. Use the simple past and any other words you see.

A: People associate American movies with Hollywood. But in the beginning, the American film industry

____wasn't based____ in Hollywood. It _____ in New York.
　　　　1. not/base　　　　　　　　　　　　　　**2. base**

B: When _____ in Hollywood?
　　　　　　3. the first film/make

A: The first Hollywood film _____ in 1911. Early movie theaters
　　　　　　　　　　　　　　　4. produce

_____ "nickelodeons."
　　5. call

B: Why _____ "nickelodeons"?
　　　　6. they/call

A: Because they cost a nickel, or five cents.

B: I wonder how else nickelodeons were different from the way theaters are today.

_____ in nickelodeons?
　　　7. snacks/sell

A: At first, food _____ at all. Then outside vendors _____ to come in
　　　　　　8. not/sell　　　　　　　　　　　　**9. permit**

and sell snacks. But when theaters owners realized that they could make money for themselves by

selling snacks, vendors _____ to come in anymore.
　　　　　　　　10. not/permit

B: What _____? Popcorn? I love eating popcorn at the movies.
　　　11. sell

A: Me too. But popcorn came later.

continued

B: I understand that early films had no sound. How did the audience know what was happening?

A: Some of the dialogue _____ on signs. And special music

                           12. show

_____ for a movie. A pianist or organist would play live music in the theater to
    13. write

create a mood. For example, dramatic music _____ for stormy
                                       14. usually/play

weather or scary scenes, and romantic music _____ for love scenes.
                                   15. use

B: When _____ to films?
              16. sound/add

A: In 1927.

B: And when _____ ?
                  17. the first color movie/make

A: The first color movies

_____ in the early
         18. actually/make

1900s, but many of these films _____ .
                       19. lost

B: How do you know so much about movies?

A: I'm majoring in film. We _____ an
                     20. give

assignment to write a paper about the early days of

the movies.

"Ha! Ha!"

Caption used in a silent film to show laughter

EXERCISE 3 Fill in the blanks with the passive voice of the verb given. Use the simple present or present continuous, as indicated.

    You have checked the movie listings online. The theater website says the movie will begin at 7:30 p.m.

You arrive at 7:00. You've bought your popcorn, and now you're ready to see your movie, right? Not so soon!

First you __<u>are shown</u>__ a number of ads for cars, soft drinks, TV shows, and more. Then you
        1. simple present: show

_____ to turn off your cell phone. Now the lights _____ and
  2. simple present: tell   **3. present continuous: dim**

the theater is becoming dark. The movie's ready to begin, right? Wrong! Next come the movie trailers.

Trailers _____ to advertise new movies that are coming soon or that _____
    4. simple present: use   **5. present continuous: show**

in other parts of the same theater. A trailer _____ to two and a half minutes, so the movie
                        6. simple present: limit

will begin soon. Right? Wrong again. Sometimes as many as five or six trailers

_____ . Again you _____ to turn off your cell phone.
  7. simple present: present   **8. simple present: ask**

    So when _____ ? Probably about 7:45. OK. Now the movie is
                9. simple present: a 7:30 movie/show

finally beginning. And guess what? Someone's cell phone always rings during the movie!

3.3 Active and Passive Voice — Use

Active: George Lucas **directed** *Star Wars.* **Passive:** *Star Wars* **was directed** by George Lucas. **Active:** Brad Pitt **will present** the next award. **Passive:** The next award **will be presented** by Brad Pitt.	When the sentence has a **strong** agent (a specific person), we can use either the active or passive voice. The passive with a strong agent is often used with the following verbs: *make, discover, invent, design, build, present, direct, write, paint, compose.* The active sentence calls attention to the subject. The passive sentence calls attention to the action or the receiver of the action.
Popcorn **was left** on the floor of the theater. The Dolby Theater **was built** in 2001.	When the sentence has a **weak** agent (identity of the agent is not important, not known, or is obvious), the passive voice is used without a *by* phrase. It would be unnecessary to say, "The theater was *built by builders.*"
Active: Do you **know** the winners' names? **Passive: The winners' names** are not known until the night of the ceremony. **Active:** The Academy presents **awards** to the best actors and directors. **Passive:** The awards **are presented** every year.	The passive voice can be used to shift the emphasis to the object of the preceding sentence.
I **was told** that you didn't like the movie.	The passive voice can be used to hide the identity of the agent.
Informal: *We* **don't know** the winners' names ahead of time. **Formal:** The winners' names **are** not **known** ahead of time. **Informal:** *They* **built** the Dolby theater in 2001. **Formal:** The Dolby theater **was built** in 2001.	In conversation, the active voice is often used with the impersonal subjects: *people, you, we,* or *they.* These are *weak* subjects. In more formal speech and writing, the passive is used with no agent.

EXERCISE 4 Some of the following sentences have a strong agent and can be changed to passive voice using the agent. Some have a weak agent and should be changed to passive voice without the agent. Change all sentences to passive voice.

1. Someone designs beautiful dresses for the actresses.

   _____ Beautiful dresses are designed for the actresses. _____

2. Prada designed Anne Hathaway's dress.

   _____ Anne Hathaway's dress was designed by Prada. _____

3. They compose music to give the movie a mood.

   _____

4. John Williams composed the music for *Star Wars*.

   _____

5. They show credits⁷ at the end of the movie.

   _____

6. They made the first Hollywood movie in 1911.

   _____

7. Someone nominates actors for the awards.

   _____

8. George Clooney presented an award.

   _____

9. You can buy movie tickets online.

   _____

10. They have sold out⁸ all the tickets.

   _____

11. Charles Cretors invented the popcorn machine.

   _____

12. They sell popcorn in movie theaters.

   _____

13. Someone gave me free tickets for the movie.

   _____

---

7 *credits:* the list of people who made a movie
8 *to sell out:* to have no more of something

EXERCISE 5 Fill in the blanks with the active or passive voice of the verb given. Use the simple present or the modal indicated.

_____Do you like_____ to watch movies in movie theaters? Well, I don't. First, movies are expensive.
    1. you/like

On Friday and Saturday nights, the movie theater is always crowded. I walk into the lobby, and it

_____ of popcorn. I am tempted to buy some, but it's so overpriced.
    2. smell

In the movie theater close to my house, there's a free parking lot. When I enter, a small ticket comes out,

but it _____ in the theater. I _____ to validate it,
    3. must/validate⁹   **4. often/forget**

so I have to pay for parking.

If I _____ for the 7 p.m. show, the tickets _____ .
    5. arrive   **6. often/sell out**

The only seats left are in the first few rows. Tickets _____ earlier online, but they're
    7. can/buy

more expensive that way.

In a theater, I have to watch movie trailers. The trailer scenes _____ from the most
    8. take

exciting parts of the film, and they're often too loud. I heard that some of these scenes

_____ specifically for the trailer and don't even appear in the film!
    9. create

I _____ to watch movies at home on my new large screen TV. With my cable service,
    10. prefer

I _____ to watch newer movies for a reasonable price. Older movies _____
    11. can/pay   **12. can/borrow**

from my local library for free. Even though DVDs _____ trailers too, they
    13. have

_____ .
    14. can/skip

When I watch a movie at home, I _____ my phone so that I _____ .
    15. turn off   **16. not/interrupt**

Sometimes I _____ my friends and we _____ popcorn in the microwave.
    17. invite   **18. make**

We _____ money and don't have any of the frustrations of going to the theater.
    19. save

EXERCISE 6 About You Underline the verbs in the following sentences. Write *P* if the verb is passive.
Write *A* if the verb is active. Work with a partner and discuss whether the statement is true in your native country.

1. Popcorn _____is sold_____ in movie theaters. P

2. Movie tickets can be bought online.

3. Several movies are shown in the same theater at the same time.

4. Movie tickets are expensive.

5. A lot of American movies are shown in my country.

continued

---

⁹ *to validate:* to approve and accept as payment

6. Actors earn a lot of money.

7. The best actors are given an award.

8. Senior citizens pay less money to see a movie.

3.4 Verbs with Two Objects

Examples	Explanation
Active: They gave Spielberg an award. I.O. D.O. **Passive 1:** Spielberg was given an award. **Passive 2:** An award was given to Spielberg.	Some verbs have two objects: a direct object (D.O.) and an indirect object (I.O.). When this is the case, the passive sentence can begin with either object. If the direct object (*an award*) becomes the subject of the passive sentence, *to* is used before the indirect object.
Language Note: Some verbs that use two objects are: bring hand offer pay send show teach write give lend owe sell serve take tell	

EXERCISE 7 Change the following sentences to passive voice in two ways. Omit the agent.

1. They gave the actress an award.

   _____The actress was given an award._____

   _____An award was given to the actress._____

2. They handed the actress an Oscar.

   _____

   _____

3. Someone will give Alex two free tickets.

   _____

   _____

4. They have sent me an invitation.

   _____

   _____

5. Someone showed us the movie.

   _____

   _____

6. They have lent the director money.

   _____

   _____

The HISTORY of ANIMATION

CD 1
TR 18

🎧 **Read the following article. Pay special attention to the words in bold.**

You have probably seen some great computer animated movies, like *Toy Story, Finding Nemo,* or *Frozen*. Computer animation **has become** the norm[10] in today's world. But animation has been around for over one hundred years. It **has changed** a lot over time. How **was** it **done** before computers **were invented**?

Early animations **were created** by hand. At the beginning of the 1900s, Winsor McCay, who **is considered** the father of animation, **worked** alone and animated his films by himself. He drew every picture separately and had them photographed, one at a time. Hundreds of photographs **were needed** to make a one-minute film. It took him more than a year and ten thousand drawings to create a five-minute animation called *Gertie the Dinosaur*. It **was shown** to audiences in theaters in 1914.

After celluloid (a transparent material) **was developed,** animation became easier. Instead of drawing each picture separately, the animator could make a drawing of the background, which **remained** motionless, while only the characters **moved**.

Walt Disney, the creator of Mickey Mouse, **took** animation to a new level. He **added** sound and music to his movies and **produced** the first full-length animated film, *Snow White and the Seven Dwarfs*. Many people think he was a great animator, but he wasn't. Instead, he **worked** mainly as a story editor. He was also a clever businessman who had other artists do most of the drawings.

Toy Story, which **came** out in 1995, was the first computer-animated film. Computer animation **was** also **used** for special effects in movies such as *Star Wars* and *Avatar*. If you've seen *Life of Pi*, you may be surprised to learn that the tiger **was done** by animation. To create the illusion[11] of movement in these films, an image[12] **was put** on the computer and then quickly **replaced** by a similar image with a small change. While this technique is similar to hand-drawn animation, the work **can be done** much faster on the computer. In fact, anyone with a home computer and special software can create a simple animation. Have you ever tried to do it?

continued

---

[10] *norm:* a common expectation
[11] *illusion:* a false idea of reality
[12] *image:* a picture or drawing

Important Dates in Animation

1914 Winsor McCay **created** the first animation on film, *Gertie the Dinosaur*.

1918 Walt Disney **opened** a cartoon studio in Kansas City, Missouri.

1923 Disney **moved** his studio to Hollywood.

1928 The first Mickey Mouse cartoon **was introduced**. It was the first talking cartoon.

1937 Disney **produced** *Snow White and the Seven Dwarfs*, the first full-length animated cartoon.

1995 *Toy Story* **became** the first full-length film animated entirely on computers.

2014 *Frozen* **won** the Academy Award for best animated film.

COMPREHENSION CHECK Based on the reading, tell if the statement is true (**T**) or false (**F**).

1. Animation was seen in movie theaters over one hundred years ago.

2. *Gertie the Dinosaur* was created by Walt Disney.

3. It's possible to create a realistic looking animal using computer animation.

3.5 Transitive and Intransitive Verbs

Examples	Explanation
verb object **Active:** McCay **created** the first animated film. **Passive:** The first animated film **was created** in 1914. verb object **Active:** Walt Disney **didn't draw** his cartoons. **Passive:** His cartoons **were drawn** by studio artists.	Most active verbs are followed by an object. They can be used in the active and passive voice. These verbs are called *transitive* verbs.
Disney **lived** in Hollywood most of his life. He **became** famous when he created Mickey Mouse. He **worked** with many artists. What **happened** to the first Mickey Mouse cartoon?	Some verbs have no object. These are called *intransitive verbs*. We don't use the passive voice with these verbs: arrive go remain be happen sleep become live stay come occur wait die rain fall recover (from illness)
Some animations **look** so real. The popcorn **smells** fresh.	The sense perception verbs are intransitive: *look, appear, feel, sound, taste, smell, seem*.

Examples	Explanation
(T) Someone **left** the DVD in the DVD player. It **was left** there last night. (I) Disney **left** Kansas City in 1923. (T) We **walked** the dog when we got home. The dog **was walked** in the morning too. (I) We **walked** to the theater near our house.	Some verbs can be transitive (T) or intransitive (I), depending on their meaning and use. A transitive verb can be active or passive. An intransitive verb can only be active.
(I) Animation **has changed** a lot since the early days. (T) The janitor **changed** the light bulb. The light bulb **was changed** last night.	*Change* and *move* can be intransitive (I) or transitive (T). When a change happens through a natural process, it is intransitive. When someone causes the change, it is transitive.
(I) In an animated movie, it looks like the characters **are moving**, but they are not. (T) The janitor **moved** the chairs. They **were moved** to another room.	*Move* can be intransitive (I) or transitive (T). When someone causes the move, it is transitive.
Walt Disney **was born** in 1901. He **died** in 1966.	We use *be* with *born*. We don't use *be* with *die*.[13]

EXERCISE 8   Read the following sentences. Find and underline the main verb in each one. Then identify which sentences can be changed to the passive voice, and change those sentences. If no change is possible, write *no change* or *NC*.

1. Winsor McCay <u>made</u> the first animated film.

   The first animated film was made by Winsor McCay.

2. Winsor McCay <u>became</u> famous for *Gertie the Dinosaur*.

   no change

3. McCay worked in Cincinnati.

   _____

4. Someone offered him a job as a newspaper artist.

   _____

5. He left Cincinnati.

   _____

continued

---

[13] *Born* is the past participle of the transitive verb *bear* (A woman *bears* children.). *Die* is an intransitive verb.

6. He moved to New York in order to work for the *New York Herald Tribune.*

_____

7. People considered the *Herald Tribune* to have the highest quality color.

_____

8. What happened to the animation *Gertie the Dinosaur*?

_____

9. Can we see it today?

_____

10. Did they preserve it?

_____

11. You can find it online.

_____

12. *Gertie the Dinosaur* seems very simple compared to today's animations.

_____

13. Animation has changed a lot over the years.

_____

14. Today they create most animation on computers.

_____

15. Someone left a good article about McCay on the table.

_____

EXERCISE 9 Circle the correct words to complete this article about Walt Disney.

Walt Disney (**was born**/born) in Chicago in 1901. He (*began*/*was begun*) drawing and painting when he
1.   2.

was a small child. When he was in high school, he (*gave*/*was given*) the job of drawing cartoons for the
3.

school newspaper. After high school, Disney (*worked*/*was worked*) for a company making commercials. At
4.

that job, he (*became*/*was become*) interested in celluloid. In 1923, Disney (*moved*/*was moved*) to California.
5.   6.

There, he (*started*/*was started*) to work on his most famous character, Mickey Mouse. We can all
7.

(*recognize*/*be recognized*) this lovable little mouse. But when Mickey (*first created*/*was first created*), he
8.   9.

(*looked*/*was looked*) different. The original cartoon mouse (*named*/*was named*) "Mortimer," not "Mickey."
10.   11.

Walt's partner (*changed*/*was changed*) Mickey's look to the character we know today.
12.

At first, Mickey Mouse animations had no sound. But in 1929, after sound (*introduced*/*was introduced*)
13.

into movies, Walt Disney (*created*/*was created*) *Steamboat Willie*, with a talking mouse and music. The
14.

cartoon was an instant success. Later new characters (*added*/*were added*): Minnie Mouse, Donald Duck,
15.

Goofy, and Pluto. In 1932, Disney's short animation *Flowers and Trees* was the first animated movie that

(*produced*/*was produced*) in color—and Disney (*won*/*was won*) his first Oscar.
16.   17.

In 1937, Disney's *Snow White and the Seven Dwarfs* was the first full-length animated film. Disney

(*earned*/*was earned*) 1.5 million dollars and (*won*/*was won*) an honorary Academy Award for that film.
18.   19.

In 1955, Disney (*built*/*was built*) Disneyland in California, which became a favorite vacation destination
20.

for families with small children. A new Disney park, called Disney World, (*was building*/*was being built*) in
21.

Florida when Disney (*died*/*was died*) in 1966. As of today, five Disney theme parks
22.

(*have built*/*have been built*) in four different countries.
23.

EXERCISE 10 Fill in the blanks with the active or passive form of the verb given. Use the past.

Ronald Reagan __was elected__ president of the United States in 1980. Before he _____
        1. elect   **2.** become

president, he was governor of California. Even before that, he _____ as a Hollywood actor.
                                                          3. work

He _____ in 53 Hollywood movies between 1937 and 1964. He _____
    4. appear   **5.** not/consider

a great actor, and he never _____ an Oscar.
                          6. win

On March 20, 1981, the day the Oscar ceremony _____ to take place, something
                                              7. schedule

terrible _____ . Reagan _____ in an assassination attempt. Fortunately, he
     8. happen   **9.** shoot

_____ from his wounds. One of his aides, who was with him at the time
   10. not/die

_____ . Out of respect for the president, the Academy Awards ceremony
  11. also/wound

_____ for one day.
  12. postpone

Reagan _____ and continued to serve as president until he _____ his
    13. recover   **14.** finish

second term in 1989. He _____ in 2004 at the age of 93.
             15. die

3.6 The Passive Voice with *Get*

Examples	Explanation

A Hollywood actor **gets paid** a lot of money. I saw a violent movie, but I didn't like it. A lot of people **got shot**.	In conversation, we sometimes use *get* instead of *be* with the passive.
	     get paid = be paid
	     get shot = be shot
	 Get is frequently used with: *shot, killed, injured, invited, wounded, paid, hired, hurt, fired, laid off, picked, caught, done, sent, stolen.*

He **was shot** by a cowboy. He **got shot** three times.	If there is an agent, we use *be*, not *get*. We usually omit the agent after *get*.
How much **do** actors **get paid** for a movie? Winsor McCay **didn't get paid** a lot of money.	When *get* is used in the simple present and the simple past, questions and negatives are formed with *do, does, did*.

EXERCISE 11 Change the following sentences to use *get* instead of *be*. If you see a *by* phrase, omit it.

1. Ronald Reagan was shot on the day of the Oscars.

   Ronald Reagan got shot on the day of the Oscars.

2. One of his aides was shot by the same man too.

   One of his aides got shot too.

3. Reagan wasn't killed by the shooter.

   _____

4. Was the aide killed by him?

   _____

5. Was the shooter caught by the police?

   _____

6. Movie stars are paid a lot of money.

   _____

7. Who will be picked for the starring role of the movie?

   _____

8. I wasn't invited to the Academy Awards.

   _____

Ronald Reagan played the role of Johnny Jones in the movie *This is the Army.*

CHARLIE CHAPLIN

🎧 Read the following article. Pay special attention to the words in bold.

CD 1
TR 19

You have seen many movies and animations with the most **advanced** technology. And you can probably recognize many of today's popular actresses and actors. But have you ever heard of Charlie Chaplin? Charlie Chaplin was one of the greatest actors in the world. During the time of silent movies, Chaplin was the highest-**paid** person in the world—not just the highest-**paid** actor. His **amusing** character, the Little Tramp, with his **worn** out shoes, round hat, and cane, is still well **known** to people throughout the world.

Chaplin had an **amazing** life. His idea for this poor tramp probably came from his childhood experiences. Born in poverty[14] in London in 1889, Chaplin was abandoned by his father and left in an orphanage[15] by his sick mother. He became **interested** in acting at the age of five. At ten, he left school to travel with a British acting company. In 1910, he made his first trip to the United States. He was talented, athletic, and **hardworking**. On his second trip to the United States, in 1912, his talent was recognized and he was offered a movie contract. In 1917, when his contract expired, he built his own studio, where he produced, directed, and wrote the movies he starred in. He even composed the music that was played with his movies. Five years after arriving in the United States, he was earning $10,000 a week.[16]

Even though sound was introduced in movies in 1927, Chaplin continued to make silent movies. He didn't make a movie with sound until 1940, when he played a comic version of the **terrifying** dictator, Adolf Hitler.

As Chaplin got older, he faced **declining** popularity as a result of his politics and personal relationships. After he left the United States in 1952, Chaplin was not allowed to re-enter because of his political views. He didn't return to the United States until 1972, when he was given a special Oscar for his lifetime of **outstanding** work.

Charlie Chaplin in his role as the Little Tramp

---

14 *poverty:* lack of money and material possessions
15 *orphanage:* a place where children without parents live and are cared for
16 In today's dollars, that amount would be close to $183,000 a week.

COMPREHENSION CHECK Based on the reading, tell if the statement is true (**T**) or false (**F**).

1. When Chaplin was 10 years old, he came to America.

2. He hired someone to compose the music for his movies.

3. He started life poor but quickly became rich.

3.7 Participles Used as Adjectives

Examples	Explanation
Today's movies use **advanced** technology. Chaplin was not an **educated** man.	Some past participles are used as adjectives.
Chaplin received an Oscar for his **outstanding** work. In later life, he faced **declining** popularity.	Some present participles are used as adjectives.
Chaplin was **extremely hardworking**. He was a **highly paid** actor.	An adverb sometimes precedes the participle.
Chaplin's life **interests** me. (*interest* = verb) (a) Chaplin's life is **interesting**. He made many **interesting** movies. (b) I am **interested** in learning more about Chaplin. Chaplin **amuses** us. (*amuse* = verb) (a) The Little Tramp was an **amusing** character. He did many **amusing** things. (b) We saw his movie and we were **amused**.	In some cases, both the present participle (a) and the past participle (b) of the same verb can be used as adjectives. The present participle (a) has an active meaning. Someone or something *actively* causes a feeling in others. The past participle (b) gives a passive meaning. It describes the person who *passively* experiences a feeling.
Chaplin played the **terrifying** dictator, Adolf Hitler. I saw a scary movie, and I was **terrified**.	A person can cause a feeling in others or can experience a feeling. Therefore, a person can be both *terrifying* and *terrified*, *interesting* and *interested*, etc.
The story about Chaplin is **interesting**. Chaplin's movies are **entertaining**.	An object (like a story or a movie) doesn't have feelings, so a past participle, such as *interested* or *entertained*, cannot be used to describe an object.

Language Note:
Some common paired participles are:

amazing	amazed	exhausting	exhausted
amusing	amused	frightening	frightened
annoying	annoyed	frustrating	frustrated
boring	bored	interesting	interested
confusing	confused	puzzling	puzzled
convincing	convinced	satisfying	satisfied
disappointing	disappointed	surprising	surprised
embarrassing	embarrassed	terrifying	terrified
exciting	excited	tiring	tired

EXERCISE 12 Use the verb in each sentence to make two new sentences. In one sentence, use the present participle. In the other, use the past participle.

1. The movie entertained us.

   The movie was entertaining.

   We were entertained.

2. Violent movies frighten children.

   _____

   _____

3. Chaplin amused the audience.

   _____

   _____

4. The adventure movie excited the audience.

   _____

   _____

5. The TV show bored me.

   _____

   _____

6. The end of the movie surprised us.

   _____

   _____

7. The movie confused her.

   _____

   _____

8. The movie terrified them.

   _____

   _____

EXERCISE 13 The following conversation is about a movie. Choose the correct participle to complete the conversation.

A: At the Oscars in 2012, a very (_interesting_/_interested_) movie called _The Artist_ won five awards, including
  1.
best picture, best director, and best actor.

B: Why was this so (_surprising_/_surprised_)? A lot of popular movies win several awards.
  2.

A: Well, the movie was filmed in black and white. It takes place in 1927. It's almost completely silent.

B: You're kidding! I'm really (_surprising_/_surprised_). Wasn't the audience (_confusing_/_confused_) about what
  3.   4.
was happening?

A: Like the silent movies made many years ago, signs were used to show what the actors were saying.

B: What's the movie about?

A: It's about an older man, George, who's a silent film star. He discovers a pretty, young actress, Peppy.

George wants his boss to give her a small part in his film. George's boss isn't (_convincing_/_convinced_) that
  5.
this is a good idea, but George insists. Peppy is very (_exciting_/_excited_) to get the part. When most movie
  6.
studios stop making silent movies in 1929, Peppy goes on to become a popular star in sound movies, but

George faces (_declining_/_declined_) popularity. He becomes (_depressing_/_depressed_). I don't want to tell you
  7.   8.
the end of the movie. If I do, you won't be (_surprising_/_surprised_) by the ending.
  9.

B: Don't worry. I'm not (_interesting_/_interested_) in seeing a silent movie. It sounds pretty (_boring_/_bored_) to me.
  10.   11.

EXERCISE 14 Fill in the blanks with the correct participle, present, or past, of the verb given.

Last night my friend and I went to see a new movie. We thought it was _____boring_____. It had a lot of
                                                                        1. bore
stupid car chases, which were not _____ at all. And I didn't like the characters. They
                                          2. excite
weren't very _____. We were pretty _____ because the reviewers said
                  3. convince   4. disappoint
it was a good movie. They said it had _____ visual effects. But for me, it wasn't
                                            5. amaze
_____ at all. I was _____ that I wasted $10 and a whole evening for
        6. interest   7. annoy
such a _____ movie. The only thing that was _____ was the popcorn.
          8. disappoint   9. satisfy

3.8 Other Past Participles Used as Adjectives

Examples	Explanation
No one knows the winners' names because the envelope is **sealed**. The **sealed** envelope will be opened on Oscar night. The new movie is **finished** now. Would you like to see the **finished** product? The theater looks **crowded**. I don't like to be in a **crowded** theater.	Some past participles can be used as adjectives after *be* or other linking verbs. They can also be used before a noun. The following past participles can be used that way: air-conditioned injured pleased broken insured prepared closed involved related concerned known sealed crowded locked used educated lost worried finished married wounded
We're **done** with the DVD. Do you want to borrow it? The actress's dress is **made** of silk. Children are not **allowed** to see some movies. Is this seat **taken**?	Other past participles come after *be*, but not usually before a noun. These past participles are used in this way: *accustomed, allowed, born, done, gone, located, made, permitted, taken* (meaning *occupied*).
That was a **well**-made movie. The theater is **extremely** crowded on Saturday night.	An adverb can precede some past participles.

EXERCISE 15 Fill in the blanks with the past participle of one of the words from the box.

educate	know	pay√	bear	take	finish
close	marry	interest	locate	worry	

1. Chaplin was a highly _____paid_____ actor.

2. Charlie Chaplin was _____ in England in 1889.

3. Was he an _____ man? Did he go to college?

4. Charlie Chaplin was _____ in making funny movies about serious topics.

5. His film studio was _____ in Hollywood.

6. He was _____ several times.

7. American actors are usually well _____ throughout the world.

8. Movie theaters are usually _____ early in the morning. They usually open around 11 a.m. or noon on weekends.

9. If you're _____ about getting a seat, you can buy your tickets beforehand online.

10. Excuse me. Is this seat _____?

11. When you're _____ with your popcorn, you should throw away the bag.

3.9 *Get vs. Be* with Past Participles and Other Adjectives

Examples	Explanation
Is Julia Roberts **married**? You're yawning. I see you *are* **bored**.	*Be* + past participle describes the status of a person over a period of time.
When did she *get* **married**? Some people *got* **bored** with the movie and walked out.	*Get* + past participle means *become*. There is no reference to the continuation of this status.
Most movie stars *are* **rich**. Chaplin *was* **old** when he received an Oscar.	*Be* + adjective describes the status of a person over a period of time.
A lot of people would like to *get* **rich** quickly. Most stars don't want to *get* **old**. They want to look young forever.	*Get* + adjective means *become*.

Past Participles with *get*			Adjectives with *get*	
get accustomed to	get dressed	get scared	get angry	get old
get acquainted	get worried	get tired	get dark	get rich
get bored	get hurt	get used to	get fat	get sleepy
get confused	get lost		get hungry	get upset
get divorced	get married			

Language Note: Notice the difference between *to be married*, *to marry*, and *to get married*.

> Meryl Streep **is married**. (*Be married* describes one's status.)
> She **married** Don Gummer in 1978. (The verb *marry* is followed by an object.)
> Meryl and Don **got married** in 1978. (*Get married* is not followed by an object.)

EXERCISE 16 Circle the correct words to complete this conversation.

A: Angelina Jolie is my favorite actress. When she (*was*/*got*) divorced, I was happy. Then she started going
                                                          1.

out with Brad Pitt and they eventually (*got married*/*married*), and I felt so sad.
                                                    2.

B: Happy? Sad? Do you think Angelina (*is*/*gets*) interested in you? She doesn't even know you! She (*is*/*gets*)
                                            3.   4.

too rich and famous to pay attention to you.

A: Well, I'm an actor too, you know. When I'm famous, Angelina will notice me if she (*gets*/*is*) single again.
                                                                                          5.

B: Well, it's possible that she'll (*get*/*be*) divorced. But you'll be an old man when, and if, you are famous. By
                                        6.

that time, she will (*be*/*get*) old, and you won't be interested in her anymore.
                       7.

A: I'll always (*get*/*be*) interested in her.
                    8.

B: Oh, really? What does your girlfriend have to say about that?

A: I never talk to her about Angelina. Once I told her how much I like Angelina, and she (*was*/*got*) angry.
                                                                                              9.

B: I don't think your girlfriend has anything to worry about.

SUMMARY OF LESSON 3

Part A Passive Voice

Passive Voice = *Be* + Past Participle	
Mickey Mouse **was created** by Walt Disney. *Star Wars* **was directed** by George Lucas.	The passive voice can be used with a strong agent if we want to emphasize the action or the receiver of the action.
Hollywood **was built** at the beginning of the twentieth century. Children **are** not **allowed** to see some movies. I **was told** that you didn't like the movie. The Oscar ceremony **is seen** all over the world.	The passive voice is usually used without an agent when: • the agent is not known, or it is not important to mention who performed the action • the agent is obvious • we want to hide the identity of the agent • the agent is not a specific person but people in general
Reagan **got shot** in 1981. No one **got killed**. Some people **got wounded**.	*Get* can be used instead of *be* in certain conversational expressions. *Get* is not used when the agent is mentioned.

Part B Participles and other Adjectives

Examples	Explanation
Silent movies are very **interesting**. Charlie Chaplin was an **entertaining** actor. Are you **interested** in the life of Charlie Chaplin? I saw a great movie and was very **entertained**.	Participles can be used as adjectives. The present participle is used to show that someone or something (silent movies; Charlie Chaplin) produced a feeling. The past participle is used to show that the subject experienced a feeling caused by someone or something else.
The movie theater is **closed**. The doors are **locked**. I don't like to see a movie in a **crowded** theater.	Other past participles are used as adjectives.
Some movie stars **get rich** quickly. Some movie stars **get married** many times.	*Get* is used with past participles and other adjectives to mean *become*.

Choose the correct form to complete the conversation.

A: Have you ever seen the movie *Life of Pi*? I'm going to watch it tonight. Do you want to watch it with me?

B: Is it a new movie?

A: No. It (*made/was made*) in 2012. I (*saw/was seen*) it once, but I'm going to (*see/be seen*) it again.
        1.   2.   3.

B: I (*don't remember/wasn't remembered*) the name. What is it about?
        4.

A: It's about a teenage boy from India. His father (*decides/is decided*) to travel with zoo animals on a ship.
                                                            5.

A storm (*is come/comes*), and the ship (*sinks/is sunk*). The boy (*survives/is survived*), but his parents
            6.   7.   8.

(*die/are died*). The boy is on a lifeboat with one of the animals, a tiger.
        9.

B: Oh, yes. Now I remember. It was a very (*interested/interesting*) movie. In some theaters it
                                                  10.

(*showed/was shown*) in 3-D. How does it end? I can't (*be remembered/remember*).
        11.   12.

A: They finally (*are arrived/arrive*) in Mexico and the tiger (*is disappeared/disappears*) and the boy
                    13.   14.

(*rescues/is rescued*).
        15.

B: For me that was a very (*disappointed/disappointing*) ending.
                                16.

A: I don't agree. The boy (*saved/got saved*) and (*lived/was lived*) to tell the story.
                            17.   18.

B: Some of the scenes with the tiger were very (*frightened/frightening*).
                                                    19.

A: The tiger wasn't real, you know. The scenes with the tiger (*did/were done*) with computer technology.
                                                                    20.

B: Really? I'm (*amazing/amazed*). Technology is so (*advanced/advancing*). Most of the story
                    21.   22.

(*happens/is happened*) when the boy is in a boat. (*Did/Was*) this movie (*make/made*) at sea?
        23.   24.   25.

A: I don't know. Probably not. So much can (*do/be done*) by computer now. I (*read/was read*) the book
                                                26.   27.

before I saw the movie. So I already (*knew/was known*) the story. But the movie (*amazed/was amazed*)
                                        28.   29.

me even more. It (*was directed/directed*) by a famous director, Ang Lee.
                    30.

B: (*Was/Did*) the movie (*nominate/nominated*) for any awards?
        31.   32.

A: Yes. It (*was/has*) nominated for many Academy Awards. So, do you want to watch it with me?
            33.

B: I don't think so. When I know how the movie (*is ended/ends*), it no longer (*interests/interesting*) me.
                                                    34.   35.

WRITING

PART 1 Editing Advice

1. Use *be*, not *do*, to make negatives and questions with the passive voice.

   The movie ~~didn't~~ **wasn't** made in Hollywood.

2. Don't use the passive voice with intransitive verbs.

   The main character ~~was~~ died at the end of the movie.

3. Don't confuse the present participle with the past participle.

   Popcorn is often ~~eating~~ **eaten** during a movie.

4. Don't forget the *-d/-ed* ending for a regular past participle.

   Music was play**ed** during silent movies.   I got bore**d** during the movie and fell asleep.

5. Don't forget to use a form of *be* in a passive sentence.

   The movie **was** seen by everyone in my family.

6. Use *by* to show the agent of the action. Use an object pronoun after *by*.

   Life of Pi was directed ~~for~~ **by** Ang Lee.   *Hulk* was directed by ~~he~~ **him** too.

7. In present and past questions and negatives, use *do* when you use *get* with the passive voice.

   My favorite movie ~~wasn't~~ **didn't** get nominated.

8. Don't forget to include a verb (usually *be*) before a participle used as an adjective.

   The movie theater **is** located on the corner of Main and Elm Streets.

9. Use *be*, not *do*, with past participles used as adjectives.

   ~~Do~~ **Are** you interested in French movies?

10. Make sure you use the correct past participle in the passive voice.

    A new movie theater is being ~~build~~ **built** near my house.

11. Don't confuse participles like *interested/interesting; bored/boring*, etc.

    I fell asleep during the ~~bored~~ **boring** movie.

12. Choose active or passive carefully.

    I ~~was~~ invited friends to watch a movie with me.   Some movies should **be seen** ~~see~~ on a large screen.

PART 2 Editing Practice

Some of the shaded words and phrases have mistakes. Find the mistakes and correct them. If the shaded words are correct, write *C*.

        One of my favorite movies is *12 Years a Slave*. This is an ~~amazing~~ ^C movie. Everyone ~~should be seen~~ *should see* it.
1. 2.

The first time I saw it, I wasn't very interested in it. The movie shown on my flight from my country to the
3. 4. 5.

United States. The screen was small and I was exhaust. I was fell asleep before the movie was ended.
6. 7. 8.

        A few months ago, a friend of mine invited me to his house to watch a movie. I surprised when
9. 10.

he told me that the movie was *12 Years a Slave*. I told him that I saw part of the movie on TV, but I

never saw the ending. I asked my friend, "Was the main character died? Or was he get rescue? Just
11. 12. 13. 14.

tell me what was happened. That's all I need to know."
15.

        "Let's watch it," my friend said. "I know you'll like it." I was agreed to watch it with him. It's
16.

based on a true story of a black man, Solomon Northup. He lived in the North and he was free, but he
17. 18.

was kidnap. He was sold into slavery in the South. He was remained a slave for 12 years. I didn't
19. 20. 21.

know much about slavery in the U.S. and I was amazed at how horrible life was for the slaves.
22.

        When I came home, I looked for more information about the movie. I looked for information on

the Internet. A lot of information can found on the film and the real person. The movie directed by
23. 24.

Steve McQueen. I wanted to find other movies directed by he too, so I googled his name. I found that
25. 26.

he directed *Shame* and *Hunger*. He also wrote the script for these movies. However, *12 Years a Slave*
27. 28.

was writing by someone else.
29.

        12 Years a Slave was nominate for several Oscars. It won for best picture of 2013. The star did a
30. 31.

great job as Solomon, but he didn't chosen as Best Actor that year. I was disappointing.
32. 33.

        Do you interested in American history? Then this movie should be seeing.
34. 35.

PART 3 Write About It

1. How are American films different from films made in your country or another country you know about? Give several examples.

2. How have movies changed over the years? Give several examples.

PART 4 Edit Your Writing

Reread the Summary of Lesson 3 and the editing advice. Edit your writing from Part 3.

TRAVEL BY
LAND
SEA and
AIR

Interior and exterior
perspective from a streetcar
traveling on St. Charles Avenue,
New Orleans, Louisiana.

The real voyage of discovery consists not in seeking new landscapes, but in having new eyes.

— Marcel Proust

TRAVEL BY LAND: The LEWIS and CLARK EXPEDITION

CD 1
TR 20

🎧 Read the following article. Pay special attention to the words in bold.

Imagine a time when most people in the eastern part of the United States had no idea what was on the other side of the Mississippi River. That was the case at the beginning of the nineteenth century, when Thomas Jefferson was the third president of the United States. The nation was only eighteen years old then and had about five million people. They **were living** between the Atlantic Ocean and the Mississippi River.

President Jefferson wanted control over the Indian tribes, who were living throughout the continent. In addition, he wanted to find a land passage to the Pacific Ocean. He **was hoping** to create a country that went from sea to sea.

Meriwether Lewis **was working** as an aide to the president. Jefferson appointed[1] Lewis and his friend William Clark to lead a dangerous, 33-man expedition[2] to the Northwest, through rivers and over the Rocky Mountains.

The expedition left St. Louis in May, 1804. As the men **were going** down the Missouri River, Clark stayed on the boat and drew maps and planned the course. Lewis often stayed on land to study animals and plants. While they **were crossing** the continent, they met some Indian tribes who were helpful. But they also met some who were hostile.[3]

A page from Clark's journal shows his drawing of a white salmon trout.

By the time the expedition reached North Dakota, winter **was** fast **approaching**. They needed to wait until spring to cross the Rocky Mountains. As they **were waiting** out the winter, they met a Shoshone[4] woman, Sacagawea, and her Canadian husband. With their help, the expedition started the most dangerous part of the journey: crossing the Rocky Mountains. They were going to need horses. Sacagawea helped them get horses from her tribe.

While they **were traveling**, they faced many hardships: hunger, danger from bears, bad weather, and uncertainty about their future. Several times, while they **were sleeping**, their horses were stolen. They had no communication with anyone back east. No one even knew if they were still alive.

In November, 1805, tired but successful, they finally made it to the Pacific. When they returned to St. Louis, almost two and a half years later, the people of St. Louis **were waiting** to greet them. They were heroes.

---

[1] *to appoint:* to choose somebody to do something
[2] *expedition:* a journey made by a group of people organized and equipped for a special purpose
[3] *hostile:* hateful, angry
[4] *Shoshone:* member of the Shoshone Indians, an American Indian tribe

COMPREHENSION CHECK Based on the reading, tell if the statement is true (**T**) or false (**F**).

1. President Jefferson's main goal was to learn about Indian life.

2. Lewis and Clark couldn't cross the mountains in the winter.

3. While traveling, they communicated with Jefferson about their location.

4.1 The Past Continuous — Form

PART A The past continuous is formed with *was* or *were* + the present participle (*-ing* form of the verb).

Subject	Was/Were (+ not)	Present Participle	Complement
I	was	reading	about Lewis and Clark.
Clark	was	making	maps.
You	were	looking	at the map of the U.S.
Lewis and Clark	were not	traveling	fast.

Language Note:

An adverb can be placed between *was/were* and the present participle.

Winter **was** *fast* **approaching**.

They **were** *probably* **getting** worried.

Clark **wasn't** *always* **riding** in the boat.

PART B Compare statements, *yes/no* questions, short answers, and *wh-* questions.

Statements	Yes/No Questions & Short Answers	Wh- Questions
They **were traveling** to the West.	**Were** they **traveling** far? Yes, they **were**.	How far **were** they **traveling**?
Lewis **wasn't making** maps.	**Was** Clark **making** maps? Yes, he **was**.	Why **wasn't** Lewis **making** maps?
Lewis **was working** for the President.	**Was** Lewis **working** in St. Louis? No, he **wasn't**.	Who else **was working** for the President?

Language Note:

The past continuous of the passive voice is *was/were* + *being* + past participle.

In 1803, preparations **were being made** for the expedition.

🎧 **EXERCISE 1** Listen to each conversation. Fill in the blanks with the words you hear.

CD 1
TR 21

1. **A:** Where ___were most Americans living___ at the beginning of the 1800s?
   a.

   B: They _____were living_____ east of the Mississippi River.
   b.

2. **A:** Lewis _____ for the president. _____ for President Jefferson at that time too?
   a.   b.

   B: No, he _____ .
   c.

3. **A:** While _____ the continent, did they meet a lot of American Indians?
   a.

   B: Yes, they did. They met a lot of American Indians while they _____ .
   b.

4. **A:** Why _____ during the winter?
   a.

   B: It was too cold. They had to wait until spring to cross the mountains.

5. **A:** Did they have any problems while _____ the mountains?
   a.

   B: Yes, they did. Sometimes at night while they _____ , their horses were stolen.
   b.

6. **A:** A Shoshone woman _____ them. How _____ them?
   a.   b.

   B: The expedition needed horses. She got horses from her tribe.

7. **A:** How many people _____ to greet them when they returned to St. Louis?
   a.

   B: Almost all of the people of St. Louis were there. They _____ to see Lewis and Clark.
   b.

4.2 The Past Continuous — Use

Examples	Explanation
In 1803, Lewis **was working** as an aide to the president. working NOW PAST ←────⊙────↑────⊙────→ FUTURE 1803	The past continuous is used to show that an action was in progress at a specific past time. It didn't begin at that time.
When they **arrived** in St. Louis, many people **were waiting** for them. *As* they **were going** down the river, Clark drew maps. *While* they **were crossing** the **continent**, they **met** many Indian tribes. crossing the continent NOW PAST ←────⊙────────⊙────→ FUTURE met Indians	We often use the simple past in one clause and the past continuous in another clause to show the relationship of a longer past action to a shorter past action. The simple past is used to express the shorter action. The past continuous is used with the longer action. *When* is used with the shorter action. *While* or *as* is used with the longer action.

Punctuation Note:

If the time clause (starting with **when, while,** or **as**) precedes the main clause, we separate the two clauses with a comma.

As they were traveling, Clark drew maps. (comma between clauses)

Clark drew maps **as** they were traveling. (no comma)

EXERCISE 2 Read this article about a space mission that took place in 2003. Pay attention to the verb forms in **bold**. If the verb form describes a longer past action, write *L* over it; if it describes a shorter past action, write *S*. Then discuss your choice with a partner.

NASA is the United States National Aeronautics and Space Administration. On January 16, 2003, NASA sent the space shuttle *Columbia* into space with seven crew members. While the *Columbia* **was going** around the Earth, the crew **conducted** science experiments. On February 1, 2003, it **was traveling** back to. Earth after completing its mission. As the *Columbia* **was flying** over east Texas just 16 minutes from its landing in Florida, it **broke** up. While families **were waiting** for the return of their relatives, they **received** the tragic news. People were shocked when they **heard** about the accident.

The causes of the disaster were studied, and this is what was found: as the *Columbia* **was lifting** off, a piece of the fuel tank **broke** off and **hit** the wing.

The *Columbia* was the second major disaster in space. The first one was in January 1986, when the space shuttle *Challenger* **exploded** while it **was lifting** off. All seven crew members were killed in that tragedy as well.

EXERCISE 3 About You Think of an important event that happened during your lifetime. Write what you were doing when you heard the news. Share your answers with a partner.

When the Soviet government fell, I was living in Kiev.

When Hurricane Sandy hit the United States, I was going to school in New York.

4.3 The Past Continuous vs. the Simple Past

Examples	Explanation
What **were** you **doing** *when* you heard the news about the *Columbia*? I **was eating** breakfast. 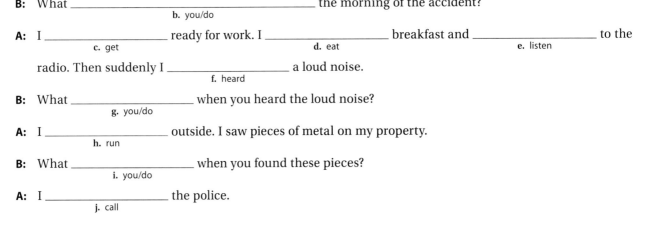	*When* can mean "at that time" or "after that time," depending on whether the past continuous or the simple past is used. The past continuous shows what was in progress *at* the time a specific action occurred.
What **did** you **do** *when* you heard the news about the *Columbia*? I **called** my friend.	The simple past shows what happened *after* a specific action occurred.
On February 1, 2003, relatives **were waiting** in Florida for the astronauts. They **were getting** ready to celebrate. Camera crews **were preparing** to take pictures of the landing.	The past continuous shows the **events leading up to** the main event **of the story**.
Suddenly, just 16 minutes before landing, the *Columbia* **broke** up.	The simple past tense shows the **main event**.

EXERCISE 4 Fill in the blanks using the words given. Use the simple past or the past continuous.

1. **A:** I remember the *Columbia* accident well. I _____was living_____ in Texas at that time.
   a. live

   B: What _____ the morning of the accident?
   b. you/do

   A: I _____ ready for work. I _____ breakfast and _____ to the
   c. get   d. eat   e. listen

   radio. Then suddenly I _____ a loud noise.
   f. heard

   B: What _____ when you heard the loud noise?
   g. you/do

   A: I _____ outside. I saw pieces of metal on my property.
   h. run

   B: What _____ when you found these pieces?
   i. you/do

   A: I _____ the police.
   j. call

2. A: Where _____ when the accident _____?
                a. the *Columbia*/go   **b.** happen

  B: It _____ to Florida.
               c. travel

  A: What _____ when the accident happened?
              d. you/do

  B: I _____ ready for school. Then my sister called me. When she _____ me about
          e. get   **f.** tell

     the accident, I _____ on the TV. When they _____ the sad faces of the relatives,
                 g. turn   **h.** show

     I _____ to cry.
         i. start

3. A: As I _____ an article on my tablet about Lewis and Clark, I _____ a word I
             a. read   **b.** find

    didn't know: "tribe."

  B: What _____ to find out the meaning?
               c. you/do

  A: I _____ my finger on the word and the definition popped up.
           d. put

EXERCISE 5 Choose the correct tense (simple past or past continuous) to complete the following conversations.

  1. A: While I (*looked/was looking*) for a movie at the library yesterday, I (*found/was finding*) a DVD about
                  a.   **b.**

     Lewis and Clark.

    B: What (*did you do/were you doing*) with it?
                     c.

    A: I (*took/was taking*) it out of the library.
            d.

  2. A: While Lewis and Clark (*crossed/were crossing*) the country with their team of 33 men, one of their men
                         a.

     (*died/was dying*).
          b.

    B: What (*did they do/were they doing*) when he died?
                      c.

    A: They (*buried/were burying*) him and continued their expedition.
                  d.

  3. A: While the teacher (*explained/was explaining*) the lesson, I (*fell/was falling*) asleep.
                       a.   **b.**

    B: What (*did the teacher talk about/was the teacher talking about*) when you fell asleep?
                        c.

    A: I think he (*talked/was talking*) about Lewis and Clark.
                 d.

    B: I can't believe you fell asleep. The story was so exciting.

    A: I thought so too. But the night before, while I (*slept/was sleeping*), the phone rang and (*woke/was waking*) me
                                      e.   **f.**

     up. When I finished talking on the phone, I (*tried/was trying*) to go back to sleep but couldn't.
                                           g.

continued

4. A: I haven't seen you for a while.

    B: I (*visited/was visiting*) my cousin in Washington, DC, all week.
                 a.

    A: Did you have a good time?

    B: Yes. We were planning to visit the Air and Space Museum, but it was closed for repair.

    A: So what (*did you do/were you doing*) instead?
                      b.

    B: We (*went/were going*) to the National Museum of the American Indian instead.
               c.

5. A: What (*did you do/were you doing*) at around eight o'clock last night? I called you and texted you,
                 a.

    but you didn't reply.

    B: I (*watched/was watching*) a documentary about American history.
               b.

    A: But I called you again around midnight. What (*did you do/were you doing*) around midnight?
                                   c.

    B: I'm sure I (*slept/was sleeping*). When I got in bed, I (*turned/was turning*) off the phone.
               d.   **e.**

TRAVEL BY SEA:
The First and Last
VOYAGE of
the *TITANIC*

A remotely operated vehicle explores the anchor of the *Titanic*.

Ken Marschall '87 ©

🎧 **Read the following article. Pay special attention to the words in bold.**

CD 1
TR 22

The year was 1912. The railroad across the United States **had** already **been built**. The Wright brothers **had** already **made** their first successful flight. Henry Ford **had** already **produced** his first car. The *Titanic*—the ship of dreams— **had** just **been built** and was ready to make its first voyage from England to America, with over two thousand people aboard.[5]

The *Titanic* was the most magnificent[6] ship that **had** ever **been built**. It had luxuries that ships **had** never **had** before: electric light, elevators, a swimming pool, libraries, and more. It was built to give its first-class passengers all the comforts of the best hotels. Some of the wealthiest people in the world were on the *Titanic*. But not everyone on the *Titanic* was rich. Most of the passengers in third class were emigrants who **had left** behind a complete way of life and were going to America with hopes of a better future.

The *Titanic* began its voyage on April 10. The previous winter **had been** unusually mild, and by spring large blocks of ice **had broken** away from the Arctic region. The captain **had been receiving** warnings about ice, but he was not very worried; he did not realize how much danger the ship was in. On April 14, at 11:40 p.m., an iceberg was spotted right ahead. The captain tried to reverse the direction of his ship, but he couldn't, because it **had been traveling** too fast. It hit the iceberg and started to sink. The *Titanic* **had** originally **had** 32 lifeboats, but 12 of them **had been removed** before sailing to make the ship look more elegant.[7] There were only enough lifeboats for about half of the people aboard.

While the ship was sinking, passengers were being put on lifeboats, women and children before men. First-class passengers boarded[8] the lifeboats before second- and third-class passengers. By the time the third-class passengers came up from their cabins, most of the lifeboats **had** already **left**, some of them half empty. Within two hours and forty-five minutes, the ship **had gone** completely down.

Cold and afraid, people in the lifeboats **had been waiting** all night, not knowing if they would be saved or if their loved ones were dead or alive. In the early morning, the *Carpathia*, a ship that responded to the *Titanic*'s call for help, arrived to rescue the survivors. Only one-third of the passengers survived.

---

[5] *aboard:* on a ship
[6] *magnificent:* very beautiful or impressive
[7] *elegant:* stylish in appearance
[8] *to board:* to enter a ship, airplane, train, etc.

COMPREHENSION CHECK   Based on the reading, tell if the statement is true (**T**) or false (**F**).

1. By the time the *Titanic* was built, the airplane had already been invented.

2. There were enough lifeboats for most of the passengers.

3. The people in lifeboats were rescued immediately.

4.4 The Past Perfect — Form

PART A   The past perfect is formed with the auxiliary verb *had* + the past participle.

Subject	Had (+ not)	Past Participle	Complement
The previous winter	**had**	**been**	mild.
Ice	**had**	**broken**	away.
The captain	**had not**	**understood**	the danger.

Language Notes:

1. Pronouns (except *it*) can be contracted with *had*: *I'd, you'd, she'd, he'd, we'd, they'd.*

     The captain knew about the ice. **He'd** had a chance to turn the ship around, but he didn't.

2. The contraction for *had not* is *hadn't.*

     He **hadn't** paid attention to the warnings.

3. Apostrophe + *d* can be a contraction for both *had* or *would.* The verb form following the contraction indicates what the contraction means.

     They'd left the ship. = They *had* left the ship.

     They'd leave the ship. = They *would* leave the ship.

4. An adverb can be placed between *had* and the past participle.

     Some passengers **had *never* been** on a ship before.

5. The past perfect of the passive voice is *had been* + past participle.

     The *Titanic* **had been built** as a luxury ship.

6. For an alphabetical list of irregular past tenses and past participles, see Appendix L.

PART B   Compare statements, *yes/no* questions, short answers, and *wh-* questions.

Statements	Yes/No Questions & Short Answers	Wh- Questions
The captain **had received** several warnings.	**Had** he **received** warnings early enough? Yes, he **had**.	How many warnings **had** he **received**?
He **hadn't realized** the danger he was in.	**Had** he **paid** attention to the warnings? No, he **hadn't**.	Why **hadn't** he **paid** attention to the warnings?
Some people **had gotten** on lifeboats immediately.	**Had** third-class passengers **gotten** on lifeboats immediately? No, they **hadn't**.	How many people **had gotten** on lifeboats?

EXERCISE 6 This is the story of a young passenger on the *Titanic*. Fill in the correct past perfect using one of the verbs from the box. If you see an adverb given, include that with the verb.

| survive | leave | jump | happen | be | take | die | say ✓ | die | meet |

Jack Thayer was a 17-year-old passenger on the *Titanic*, traveling with his parents.

He ___had just said___ goodnight to his parents and was getting ready to go to bed when he felt a bump.
　　　1. just

He and his father went out to see what _____. At first, the passengers remained
　　　　　　　　　　　　　　　　　　　　　　　2.

calm. But one of the ship's designers, whom the Thayers _____ several times during
　　　　　　　　　　　　　　　　　　　　　　　　　　　　　3.

the short voyage, told them that the *Titanic* would not last an hour.

Passengers were trying to get on the lifeboats, but many lifeboats _____ half
　　　　　　　　　　　　　　　　　　　　　　　　　　　　4. already

full. Thayer got separated from his parents. As the ship was sinking, he jumped into the icy water and swam

to an overturned boat. He heard the cries of passengers who _____ into the icy
　　　　　　　　　　　　　　　　　　　　　　　　　　　　5.

waters. Thayer spent the night not knowing if his parents were dead or alive. In the morning, the passengers

in the lifeboats were rescued by the *Carpathia*. It was then that he learned that his mother

_____ but, unfortunately, his father _____.
　　　6.　　　　　　　　　　　　　　　　　　　　　　　　　　7.

Thirty years later, he wrote his story about that tragic night. But his account was never published. He

made five hundred copies and gave them to family and friends. In April, 2012, on the one hundredth

anniversary of the tragedy, his notebooks were published. They contain his story of what

_____ place that night.
　　　8.

Jack Thayer faced another tragedy in his life. His son, who _____ a fighter pilot,
　　　　　　　　　　　　　　　　　　　　　　　　　　　　　　　9.

was killed in World War II. This was an especially sad time for him because his mother

_____ the same year. Shortly afterward, Jack committed suicide at the age of 50,
　　　10.

which was the same age his father was when he died in 1912.

4.5 The Past Perfect — Use (Part 1)

When showing the time relationship between past events, the past perfect is used to show the event that took place first.

Examples	Explanation
By April, 1912, large blocks of ice **had broken** away from the Arctic region. **By the age of fifty**, Jack Thayer **had lost** several loved ones.	The past perfect can be used with *by* + a time reference. The past perfect shows that something occurred before that time. NOW lost loved ones PAST ← ✖ ✖ → FUTURE 50 years old
Time Clause **By the time** the rescue ship **arrived**, Main Clause most passengers **had already died**. Main Clause I **had** never **heard** of the *Titanic* Time Clause **until** I **read** the article about it today.	The past perfect can be used in a sentence with a time clause. The time clause shows the later past event and uses the simple past. The main clause shows the earlier past event and uses the past perfect. NOW rescue ship arrived PAST ← ✖ ✖ → FUTURE passengers died
When Jack's family got on the *Titanic*, they **had *never* been** on such a luxurious trip **before**. When Jack was rescued in the morning, he **hadn't *yet* learned** of his father's death.	*Never … before* or *not … yet* can be used in the main clause to emphasize the earlier time.
The ship **had been** at sea **for five days** when it hit an iceberg.	The past perfect can be used in the main clause with *for* + a time period to show the duration of the earlier past action.
Before he **jumped** in the water, he **(had) put** on his lifejacket. Many years **before** he **died**, he **had written** his personal story and **had given** copies to family and friends.	In sentences with a time clause that begins with *before* or *after*, the past perfect is optional in the main clause. Often the simple past is used in both clauses. The past perfect is more common if the earlier event does not immediately precede the later one.
It **was** 1912. The railroad **had already been** built.	We can start with a past sentence and follow it with a past perfect sentence to go further back in time.

Language Note:

Time clauses begin with *by the time, when, until*, etc.

EXERCISE 7 Fill in the blanks with the simple past or the past perfect of the verb given.

1. By 1912, the airplane ___had already been invented___ .
   passive: already/invent

2. By the time the *Titanic* _____ England, some of the lifeboats _____
   a. leave   b. passive: remove

   to make the ship look more elegant.

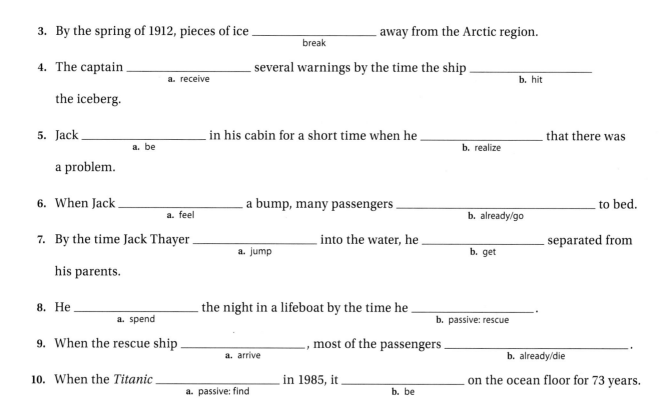

3. By the spring of 1912, pieces of ice _____ away from the Arctic region.

break

4. The captain _____ several warnings by the time the ship _____

a. receive   b. hit

   the iceberg.

5. Jack _____ in his cabin for a short time when he _____ that there was

a. be   b. realize

   a problem.

6. When Jack _____ a bump, many passengers _____ to bed.

a. feel   b. already/go

7. By the time Jack Thayer _____ into the water, he _____ separated from

a. jump   b. get

   his parents.

8. He _____ the night in a lifeboat by the time he _____ .

a. spend   b. passive: rescue

9. When the rescue ship _____ , most of the passengers _____ .

a. arrive   b. already/die

10. When the *Titanic* _____ in 1985, it _____ on the ocean floor for 73 years.

a. passive: find   b. be

EXERCISE 8 Read the sentences below. Decide which time or event took place first. Write *1* above the first action or event and *2* above the second.

1. When the Lewis and Clark expedition traveled [2] to the west, no one had done [1] it before.

2. They finally entered [2] a territory that no white man had ever entered [1] before.

3. It was 1803. For almost 20 years, President Jefferson had thought about sending an expedition to the west.

4. The expedition had traveled more than six hundred miles by the end of July.

5. Up to this time, most of the trip had been done by boat.

6. Lewis and Clark were the first white Americans to go west of the Rocky Mountains. But these lands had been occupied by native people for a long time.

7. Many American Indians had never seen a white man before they met Lewis and Clark.

8. Only one man had died by the end of the expedition.

9. He had died long before the expedition ended.

10. They returned to St. Louis, almost two and one-half years after they had left.

4.6 *When* with the Simple Past or the Past Perfect

Sometimes *when* means *after*. Sometimes *when* means *before*.

Examples	Explanation
When Jack Thayer was rescued, he **found** his mother. **When** Jack Thayer was rescued, he **had been** in a lifeboat all night.	If the simple past is used in the main clause, *when* means **after**. If the past perfect is used in the main clause, *when* means **before**.

EXERCISE 9 Fill in the blanks with the correct form of the verb given. Use the simple past to show that *when* means *after*. Use the past perfect to show that *when* means *before*.

1. When people saw the *Titanic* for the first time, they _____had never seen_____ such a magnificent ship before.

    never/see

2. When the ship was built, people _____were_____ amazed at how beautiful it was.

    be

3. When the ship left England, twelve lifeboats _____ .

    passive: remove

4. When the weather got warmer, pieces of ice _____ to break away.

    start

5. When the ship hit an iceberg, the captain _____ several warnings.

    receive

6. When Jack Thayer felt a bump, he _____ to investigate.

    go

7. When the passengers heard a loud noise, they _____ to get on the lifeboats.

    run

8. When the *Titanic* sank, a rescue ship _____ to pick up the survivors.

    come

9. When Thayer died, he _____ several tragedies in his life.

    have

10. When he died, his notebooks _____ .

    passive: not/yet/ publish

11. When his notebooks were published, people _____ more about what had happened that night.

    learn

12. When I saw the movie *Titanic*, I _____ my friends about it.

    tell

13. When I saw the movie *Titanic*, I _____ of this ship before.

    never/hear

4.7 The Past Perfect—Use (Part 2)

Examples	Explanation
Many people **died** *because* the lifeboats **had left** half empty. Jack **survived** *because* he **had jumped** into the water and **swum** to a lifeboat.	The past perfect is often used in a *because* clause to show that something happened before the verb in the main clause.
The captain **didn't realize** that his ship **had come** so close to an iceberg. Until he was rescued, Jack **didn't know** that his mother **had survived**.	The past perfect can be used in a noun clause when the main verb is past. (A noun clause begins with *know that, think that, realize that,* etc.)*
The *Titanic* **was** *the most* magnificent ship that **had** *ever* **been** built. The sinking of the *Titanic* **was** one of *the worst* transportation tragedies that **had** *ever* **happened**.	In a past sentence with the superlative form, the past perfect is used with *ever*.
One of the ship's designers, *whom* the Thayer family **had met**, **told** them that the ship would not last an hour.	The past perfect can be used in an adjective clause. (An adjective clause begins with *who, that, which, whom,* or *whose.*)**

*For more about noun clauses, see Lesson 10.

**For more about adjective clauses, see Lesson 7.

EXERCISE 10 Complete each sentence by circling the correct verb form. Use both the simple past and the past perfect in the same sentence.

1. Jack Thayer and his father (*went*/*had gone*) to investigate because they (*felt*/*had felt*) a bump.

 a.   b.

2. Jack, who (*got*/*had gotten*) separated from his parents, (*jumped*/*had jumped*) into the water and was

            a.   b.

 picked up by a lifeboat.

3. Some people in the lifeboats (*reported*/*had reported*) that they (*heard*/*had heard*) music as the ship

                                     a.   b.

 was going down.

4. Jack was seventeen years old. Losing his father (*was*/*had been*) the worst thing that

                                                    a.

 (*ever happened*/*had ever happened*) to him at that time.

                     b.

5. Later, Jack (*became*/*had become*) very depressed because his son and his mother (*died*/*had died*)

             a.   b.

 in one year.

6. People (*didn't know*/*hadn't known*) Jack Thayer's story because he (*didn't publish*/*hadn't published*) it.

                a.   b.

7. Jack's family (*knew*/*had known*) about his story because he (*gave*/*had given*) them copies of it.

                a.   b.

8. His story, which he (*wrote*/*had written*) in the 1940s, (*wasn't*/*hadn't been*) published until after his death.

             a.   b.

EXERCISE 11 Fill in the blanks with the simple past or the past perfect of the verbs given and any other words you see. Use both tenses in each item.

1. Lewis and Clark _____entered_____ a land that no
   a. enter

   white man _had ever entered_ .
   b. ever/enter

2. The expedition to the west _____ one of
   a. be

   the most dangerous journeys that men

   _____ at that time.
   b. ever/do

3. During the winter, they _____ busy
   a. keep

   writing reports about what they _____ .
   b. see

4. During the winter, they _____ equipment
   a. repair

   that _____ damaged.
   b. become

5. They _____ grizzly bear territory. The
   a. enter

   American Indians _____ them
   b. warn

   about these dangerous animals, but they thought it

   wouldn't be a problem because they had rifles. They were wrong. The grizzly bear _____
   c. be

   one of the most frightening animals they _____ .
   d. ever/see

6. On November 7, 1805, they saw a body of water. They _____ that they
   a. think

   _____ the Pacific Ocean. They were disappointed to learn that what they saw was just
   b. reach

   a river.

7. Lewis and Clark _____ the first white men to travel to the west, but these lands
   a. be

   _____ by American Indians.
   b. passive: already/occupy

EXERCISE 12 About You Fill in the blanks and discuss your answers with a partner. Talk about travel or transportation.

1. Until I was _____ , I had never _____ before.

2. By the time I was _____ years old, I _____ already

   _____ .

4.8 The Past Perfect Continuous — Form

PART A The past perfect continuous is formed with *had been* + the present participle.

Subject	Had (+ not)	Been	Present Participle	Complement
The *Titanic*	**had**	**been**	**crossing**	the Atlantic Ocean.
Jack Thayer	**had**	**been**	**waiting**	all night.
The captain	**had not**	**been**	**paying**	close attention.

Language Note:

An adverb can be placed between *had* and *been*.

Jack **had *probably* been thinking** of his parents all night.

PART B Compare statements, *yes/no* questions, short answers, and *wh-* questions.

Statements	Yes/No Questions & Short Answers	Wh- Questions
The *Titanic* **had been crossing** the Atlantic.	**Had** the ship **been crossing** in the winter? No, it **hadn't**.	How long **had** it been **traveling**?
The captain **hadn't been listening** to the warnings.	**Had** he **been traveling** too fast? Yes, he **had**.	Why **hadn't** the captain **been listening** to the warnings?
Lewis and Clark **had been traveling** for several years.	**Had** American Indians **been traveling** with Lewis and Clark? Yes, they **had**.	Which American Indians **had been traveling** with them?

EXERCISE 13 Fill in the blanks with the verb forms you hear.

CD 1
TR 23

Millvina Dean was only a nine-month-old baby when her family took her on the *Titanic*. Mr. and Mrs.

Dean _____ in third class with Millvina and her two-year-old brother.
　　　　　　　　　　1.

Millvina's father _____ a business in London for several years when an
　　　　　　　　　　　　　　2.

American cousin invited him to help run his business in the U.S. But, unfortunately, that wasn't going to

happen. Millvina, her mother, and brother were rescued, but Mr. Dean _____. A week after
　　　　　　　　　　　　　　　　　　　　　　　　　　　　3.

arriving in the United States, Millvina, her mother, and brother returned to England. For many years,

Millvina _____ about her experience because, of course, she couldn't remember
　　　　　4.

anything. What she knew she _____ from her mother. Millvina
　　　　　　　　　　　　　　5.

_____ a quiet life for many years until 1985, when the *Titanic* was found. For the
　　　6.

next twenty years she was invited to *Titanic*-related events in the United States, England, and other

countries. When she died in 2009 at the age of ninety-seven, she had been the oldest and last survivor.

4.9 The Past Perfect Continuous — Use

Examples	Explanation
The *Titanic* **had been traveling** *for* four days when it **hit** an iceberg. Millvina **had been living** a quiet life *for* many years when the *Titanic* **was found**.	The past perfect continuous is used with a continuous action that was completed before another past action (in the simple past). The duration of the continuous action is expressed with *for*.
Lewis **had known** Clark for almost ten years by the time the expedition **began**. By the time the rescue ship **arrived**, most of the passengers of the *Titanic* **had** already **died**.	We use the past perfect, not the past perfect continuous, with: nonaction verbs* actions of little or no duration

* For a list of nonaction verbs, see page 16.

EXERCISE 14 Fill in the blanks with the simple past or the past perfect continuous of the words given. Use the passive where indicated.

1. When she _____*died*_____ , Millvina Dean ___*had been living*___ in a nursing home for several years.
   a. die   b. live

2. Lewis _____ for President Jefferson for two years when the president
   a. work

   _____ him for the expedition.
   b. choose

3. Lewis and Clark _____ for three months by the time they
   a. travel

   _____ American Indians.
   b. meet

4. When Lewis and Clark finally _____ the Pacific Ocean, they
   a. see

   _____ the continent for one and a half years.
   b. cross

5. By the time Jack Thayer _____ his story, he _____
   a. write   b. think

   about this tragedy for thirty years.

6. By the time Jack Thayer _____ , he _____
   a. passive: rescue   b. hold on

   to a lifeboat all night.

7. By the time the *Titanic* _____ , it _____
   a. passive: find   b. rest

   on the ocean floor for over seventy years.

8. When the space shuttle *Columbia* _____ , it _____
   a. explode   b. travel

   for sixteen days.

EXERCISE 15 The following is a student's account of leaving her country and immigrating to the United States. Fill in the blanks with the simple past or the past perfect continuous of the verbs given.

1. When I _____ *came* _____ to the U.S., I _*had been studying*_ English for three years.

a. come   b. study

2. I _____ for two years when I _____ a chance to

a. wait   b. get

leave my country.

3. I _____ in the same house all my life when I _____

a. live   b. leave

my city.

4. I _____ very sad when I left my job because I _____

a. feel   b. work

with the same people for ten years.

5. I _____ to be a nurse for six months when a war _____

a. study   b. break out

in my country.

6. When I _____ my country, the war _____ for three years.

a. leave   b. go on

7. My family _____ in Germany for three months before we

a. wait

_____ permission to come to the U.S.

b. get

8. By the time I _____ to the U.S., I _____ for four days.

a. get   b. travel

4.10 The Past Perfect (Continuous) vs. the Present Perfect (Continuous)

The past perfect (continuous) and the present perfect (continuous) cannot be used interchangeably.

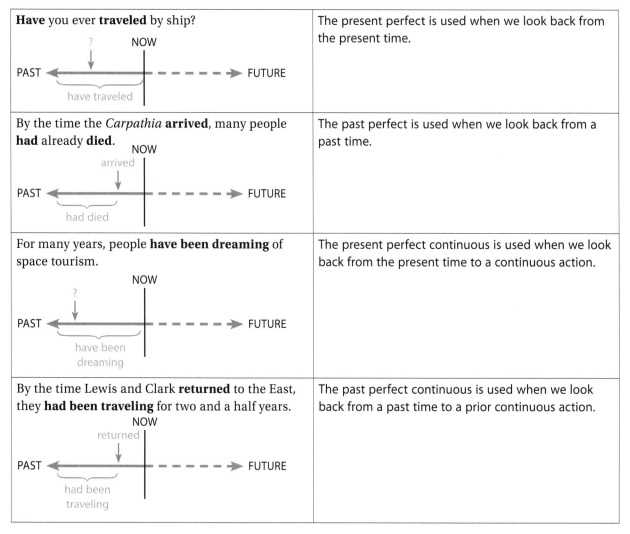

Have you ever **traveled** by ship?	The present perfect is used when we look back from the present time.
By the time the *Carpathia* **arrived**, many people **had** already **died**.	The past perfect is used when we look back from a past time.
For many years, people **have been dreaming** of space tourism.	The present perfect continuous is used when we look back from the present time to a continuous action.
By the time Lewis and Clark **returned** to the East, they **had been traveling** for two and a half years.	The past perfect continuous is used when we look back from a past time to a prior continuous action.

EXERCISE 16 Fill in the blanks with the present perfect, the present perfect continuous, the past perfect, or the past perfect continuous of the verb given. Include any other words you see.

A: I'm reading a great article about travel to Mars.

B: I didn't know that you liked to read about space exploration. How long ___*have you been*___
$\underset{\text{1. you/be}}{}$

interested in it?

A: I _____ interested in it. When I was a child, we lived in Washington, DC,
$\underset{\text{2. always/be}}{}$

but I _____ to the Air and Space Museum there. I
$\underset{\text{3. never/be}}{}$

_____ to go there, but my parents were too busy to take me. My fifth
$\underset{\text{4. always/want}}{}$

grade class _____ space exploration for three weeks when my teacher
$\underset{\text{5. study}}{}$

decided to take us to the museum. That school trip really got me interested in exploration. Lately I

_____ interested in other kinds of exploration too, like the Lewis and Clark expedition.
$\underset{\text{6. become}}{}$

_____ the Ken Burns movie about it?
$\underset{\text{7. you/ever/see}}{}$

B: I _____ of Ken Burns. Who is he?
$\underset{\text{8. never/hear}}{}$

A: He is a documentary filmmaker. He _____ a lot of interesting historical
$\underset{\text{9. make}}{}$

documentaries. I _____ many of them.
$\underset{\text{10. see}}{}$

B: I _____ to the movies lately.
$\underset{\text{11. not/be}}{}$

A: Oh. You can get his documentaries on DVD. The Lewis and Clark documentary is a long one. I started

watching it last Sunday, and I _____ it all week. When I'm finished with
$\underset{\text{12. watch}}{}$

it, you can borrow it.

B: Why do you think it's so interesting?

A: According to Ken Burns, the Lewis and Clark expedition was even more dangerous than a trip to the

moon. In fact, it was one of the most dangerous expeditions that _____
$\underset{\text{13. passive: ever/make}}{}$

at that time. The expedition _____ for two and a half years without any
$\underset{\text{14. travel}}{}$

communication with anyone back home. No one knew if they were dead or alive.

B: Sounds interesting. I think I'll borrow that DVD from you.

The DC-3, Smithsonian National Air and Space Museum, Washington, DC

TRAVEL BY AIR: The **DC-3**

CD 1
TR 24

🎧 Read the following article. Pay special attention to the words in bold.

An American Airlines airplane **left** the Newark Airport for Glendale, California. By the time the plane **arrived** in California, the passengers **had been traveling** for 18 hours and 40 minutes—and they **had made** several stops. This was an amazing flight.

Amazing? 18 hours? Several stops? Well, this **happened** in 1938. In the early days of aviation, airplanes **had been used** primarily in the military and to deliver mail. But airlines, hoping to make money, **were trying** to attract passengers away from train travel. The DC-3 airplane **changed** the airline industry and **started** to attract more and more passengers.

Before this time, a flight from New York to Los Angeles **had taken** 25 hours and **had required** 15 stops and several changes of plane. But the DC-3 **made** a number of improvements and **was** the first passenger plane to make money. However, air travel was not for everyone. A round trip, coast-to-coast flight **cost** $300, which is the equivalent of about $5,000 today.

But this **wasn't** the first passenger flight. Before the DC-3, Boeing **had built** another passenger airplane. United Airlines **bought** 60 of those airplanes, which **carried** 10 passengers and **flew** at 155 miles per hour.[9] But it **wasn't** a very attractive alternative to taking the train, even for those who could afford it. Passengers **became** dizzy,[10] and some even **fainted**. Most people **considered** the airplane to be unsafe. In fact, a famous football player **had been killed** in a plane crash over Kansas in 1931.

If airlines **wanted** to attract passengers away from train travel, they **had** to become safer, faster, and more comfortable. The 1930s **was** one of the most innovative[11] periods in aviation history. Airplanes **became** lighter, which made them go faster. The noise level **was reduced**, and the air became easy to breathe.

Since the 1930s, airline travel **has been improving**. As more and more passengers **started** seeking air travel, even greater advances **were made**. More powerful jet engines **have made** it possible to carry hundreds of passengers thousands of miles quickly. And advanced radar systems **have allowed** air traffic controllers a way of safely separating the flow of traffic.

Airplanes, which are now the preferred means of travel, won their competition with trains. Today the original DC-3 hangs in the Smithsonian National Air and Space Museum in Washington, DC.

---

9   This equals 250 kilometers per hour.
10 *dizzy:* lightheaded, faint
11 *innovative:* showing new ideas or improvements

COMPREHENSION CHECK Based on the reading, tell if the statement is true (**T**) or false (**F**).

1. The DC-3 was the first passenger plane.

2. Early airplanes were used mostly for the military and mail.

3. At first, passengers were afraid of airplane travel.

4.11 Comparison of Past Tenses

Examples	Explanation
The airplane **left** Newark on December 17, 1938. The trip **took** more than 18 hours. It **made** several stops.	The **simple past** is used for: • a short action • a long action • a repeated action
In the 1930s, airlines **were trying** to attract passengers. In 1931, Flight 599 **was flying** over Kansas when it **crashed**.	The **past continuous** shows that: • something was in progress at a specific time in the past • a longer past action (*was flying*) relates to a shorter past action (*crashed*)
By the time the airplane **landed** in California, it **had made** several stops.	The **past perfect** shows how an earlier action relates to a later past action (simple past). earlier = *had made*; later = *landed*
Passengers **had been traveling** *for* more than eighteen hours when they **landed** in California.	The **past perfect continuous** shows how an earlier continuous action relates to a later past action (simple past). *For* is used to show the duration of the continuous action. earlier = *had been traveling*; later = *landed*
Jet engines **have made** it possible to carry hundreds of passengers thousands of miles.	The **present perfect** looks back from the present time.
We're reading about transportation. **We've been reading** about it for two days.	The **present perfect continuous** looks back from the present time to a continuous action that is still happening.

Language Notes:

1. Sometimes the past continuous and the past perfect continuous can be used in the same case. The past perfect continuous is more common with a *for* phrase.

    The airplane **was flying** over Kansas when it crashed.
    The airplane **had been flying** for one hour when it crashed.

2. Sometimes the simple past or the past perfect can be used in the same case.

    Before the plane arrived in California, it **made** several stops.
    Before the plane arrived in California, it **had made** several stops.

3. Remember: We don't use the continuous form with nonaction verbs.

🎧 **EXERCISE 17** Complete the article about Henry Ford and his Model T car with the verb forms you hear.

CD 1
TR 25

When Henry Ford was born in 1863, most people _____ _were living_ _____ on farms and
                                                        1.

_____ far from home. They _____ on foot, by bicycle, or on
            2.   **3.**

horseback. By the end of the 19th century, the railroad _____,
                                                                              4.

so when it _____ necessary to go a longer distance, people _____
                    5.   **6.**

trains. Henry Ford had other ideas. Some people think Henry Ford _____ the car.
                                                                              7.

But he didn't. By the time Henry Ford _____ producing cars, the car
                                                  8.

_____ invented. At first, the car was considered an expensive toy for the rich and
          9.

_____ a "pleasure car." But Ford _____ to think about
          10.   **11.**

producing a car for middle income people. He realized that other companies _____
                                                                                          12.

their products in large numbers and were able to sell them more cheaply. By 1913, Ford

_____ the moving assembly line[12] for automobiles. With this method, he
          13.

_____ able to produce cars faster and cheaper. When workers complained that their
          14.

job was very repetitive and boring, Ford _____ their salaries. Ford was able to keep
                                                      15.

his workers happy and mass produce the Model T Ford. As a result of mass production, prices

_____ and sales _____ . During the 1920s, the term
          16.   **17.**

"pleasure car" _____ as it was being replaced by the term "passenger car."
                              18.

EXERCISE 18 Read each conversation. Fill in the blanks with the correct tense of the verbs given. Use
the passive voice and the adverbs where indicated. In some cases, more than one answer is possible.

1. **A:** _Have you ever heard_ of Henry Ford?
          a. you/ever/hear

   B: Of course, I have. He _____ the car.
                                      b. invent

   A: No, he didn't. He _____ cars in large numbers and lowered the price.
                                    c. produce

   B: Oh. I _____ that. I have a Ford car. I _____ Ford cars
                    d. not/know   **e.** drive

   for many years. The Ford _____ my favorite car.
                                    f. always/be

   A: I _____ an American car. I _____ Japanese cars.
              g. never/have   **h.** always/prefer

---

[12] *assembly line:* process in which different people add parts
of a product in sequence until the product is complete

2. A: My grandmother _____ me her car as a graduation present last month. She

                         a. give

_____ for almost 50 years when she _____ to

        b. drive   c. decide

stop. Her eyesight isn't so good anymore. Two months ago she _____ a bike and

                                             d. buy

she _____ her bike, around the neighborhood. Ever since she

      e. ride

_____ to ride her bike, her health _____ .

      f. start   g. improve

B: But how does she go long distances?

A: Since she stopped driving, everyone in the family _____ her.

                                            h. help

3. A: _____ successful?

                   a. space missions/always /be

B: They _____ successful until 1986 when the first accident _____ .

         b. be   c. occur

A: What about now? Are there still space missions?

B: No. The last space mission _____ in 2011.

                                 d. be

continued

Henry Ford is driving his Model T car, accompanied by Thomas Edison (back seat) and John Burroughs.

4. A: How did Ford learn so much about machines?

B: He _____ about machines while he _____ for other
a. learn   b. work

people. He was happy while he _____ new things, but he
c. learn

_____ bored when there was nothing new to learn.
d. become

5. A: The first cars were called "pleasure cars."

B: Why _____ "pleasure cars"?
a. passive: they/call

A: They were very expensive, and only rich people _____ them. They _____
b. have   c. passive: use

more for pleasure than for transportation.

6. A: While Ford _____ how other machines were produced, he suddenly
a. study

_____ how to produce his cars more cheaply.
b. realize

B: What _____ when he _____ this?
c. he/do   d. realize

A: He _____ the assembly line for mass-producing cars.
e. develop

7. A: I _____ the story about Lewis and Clark last week. I really enjoyed it.
a. read

B: Me too. I didn't realize that no one _____ the mountains before.
b. ever/cross

A: By the time they returned from the West, only one man on the expedition _____ .
c. die

B: That's amazing, isn't it?

8. A: Lately I _____ about buying a car. I'm tired of using public
a. think

transportation. Do you have any suggestions for me?

B: _____ a car before?
b. you/ever/buy

A: No. This is my first time.

B: _____ at a consumer magazine?
c. you/look

A: What's a consumer magazine?

B: It's a magazine that gives all kinds of information about buying a car.

_____ about what kind of car you want?
d. you/think

A: I want a small car less than five years old.

9. A: Do you know anything about the history of the *Titanic*?

B: Yes. In 1912, it was the most magnificent ship that _____.
                                             a. passive: ever/build

A: So what went wrong?

B: It _____ too fast when it _____ an iceberg and
              b. travel   **c.** hit

_____ to sink. Passengers wanted to get on lifeboats, but many of the lifeboats
         d. start

_____.
         e. already/leave

EXERCISE 19 About You Write three or more sentences about a trip you took. Try to use the different past tenses.

1. <u>While I was traveling to Los Angeles, my car broke down. While a mechanic was fixing</u>
   <u>my car, I had to stay in a hotel for a few days. When they fixed my car, I continued</u>
   <u>my trip.</u>

2. _____

   _____

3. _____

   _____

4. _____

   _____

SUMMARY OF LESSON 4

Present Perfect (relates the past to the present)

So far, we **have read** three stories about transportation.
Have you **taken** any trips lately?
Ordinary citizens **haven't traveled** into space yet.
I have a driver's license now. I **have had** my license for three months.

Present Perfect Continuous (relates past to present)

We **have been reading** about transportation for three days.
Ever since we started this lesson, I **have been thinking** about taking a trip.
Is your son driving to California now? How long **has** he **been driving**?
We**'ve been learning** a lot about travel in the past few days.

Simple Past

Lewis and Clark **crossed** the Rocky Mountains on horseback.
They **returned** from the West two and a half years later.
They **were** very brave.
They **made** their expedition over two hundred years ago.

Past Continuous

While the *Titanic* **was crossing** the Atlantic, it hit an iceberg.
Jack Thayer **was getting** ready for bed when he felt a bump.
At 11:40 p.m. many passengers **were sleeping**.

Past Perfect

When Millvina Dean died in 2009, all the other *Titanic* survivors **had** already **died**.
In 1912, the *Titanic* was the most magnificent ship that **had** ever **been built**.
To make the *Titanic* look more elegant, lifeboats **had been removed**.
By the time the DC-3 airplane reached California, it **had made** several stops.

Past Perfect Continuous

By the time the DC-3 airplane reached California, passengers **had been traveling** for more than eighteen hours.
The *Titanic* **had been traveling** for four days when it hit an iceberg.

TEST/REVIEW

Fill in the blanks with the correct form of the verbs given. Use the simple past, past continuous, present perfect, present perfect continuous, past perfect, or past perfect continuous. In some cases, more than one answer is possible.

A: I'm looking at a cool website, FlightAware.com. Do you want to see it?

B: I _'ve never_ _____ heard of it. What's it for?
   1. never / hear

A: You can track a flight. My sister left for Poland last night. I can see when her plane _____,
   2. depart

   how long it _____ , and where it is right now.
   3. fly

B: _____ yet?
   4. she/arrive

A: Not yet. She _____ in Frankfort this morning and _____
   5. arrive   **6.** change

   planes for Warsaw.

B: How many times _____ this website?
   7. you/use

A: My family and I _____ it many times. While I _____ from Boston
   8. use   **9.** travel

   to Miami last month, my family _____ it. That was an awful trip.
   10. use

B: Why? What _____ wrong?
   11. go

A: I _____ a connection in Chicago, but my plane from Boston was two hours late. So I
   12. have

   _____ my connection. The airline _____ me on another flight. By the
   13. miss   **14.** put

   time I _____ to Miami, I _____ for fourteen hours.
   15. get   **16.** travel

   Then I waited an hour for my luggage and all the other passengers _____ their
                                                                        17. get

   luggage and left, but mine didn't arrive.

B: What _____ ?
   18. you/do

A: I went to the luggage claim desk. They _____ me that they would do a search.
                                          19. tell

B: So _____ it?
   20. they/find

A: Yes. But by the time they _____ it, I _____ in
   21. find   **22.** already/be

   Miami for a week. I _____ my brother, and, luckily, we are the same size, so he
   23. visit

   _____ me his clothes to wear. Wait a minute. I see that my sister's plane
   24. give

   _____ . Look. It _____ down five minutes ago.
   25. just/arrive   **26.** touch

B: That's a cool website. I'm going to use it. I _____ the app.
                                               27. already/download

   I _____ it while you _____ it to me.
   28. do   **29.** show

WRITING

PART 1 Editing Advice

1. The simple past, active voice, does not use an auxiliary.

   The plane ~~was~~ arrived at 6:44 a.m.

2. Don't forget *be* in a past continuous sentence. Don't forget the *-ing*.

   was
   The *Titanic* ∧crossing the Atlantic when it hit an iceberg.

   ing
   While I was read∧about the airplane, I came across some new words

3. Don't forget *have* with perfect tenses.

   have
   We ∧been learning about transportation for three days.

4. Use *when*, not *while*, for an action that has no continuation.

   when
   Jack was getting ready for bed ~~while~~ he felt a bump.

5. Choose the correct past tense.

   had
   When I started this lesson, I ~~have~~ never heard of Lewis and Clark before.

   have
   My trip to the U.S. from Japan last year was the longest trip I ~~had~~ ever taken.

   sank
   The *Titanic* ~~was sinking~~ over one hundred years ago.

   came
   She has had her car ever since she ~~has come~~ to the U.S.

6. Don't confuse the *-ing* form with the past participle.

   been
   Jack had never ~~being~~ on a ship before.

7. Don't use the simple present or the present continuous for an action that began in the past. Use the present perfect or present perfect continuous.

   has been
   The airplane ~~is~~ the most popular means of travel for many years.

   has been
   She ~~is~~ working as a pilot since 2012.

PART 2 Editing Practice

Some of the shaded words and phrases have mistakes. Find the mistakes and correct them. If the shaded words are correct, write *C*.

A few years ago, I ~~was~~ saw a TV program on the one hundredth anniversary of the *Titanic*
                    1.
C
tragedy. It was a fascinating program about the survivors. I been interested in learning more about
        2.   3.

the survivors ever since I have seen it. So I started to read more about it.
              4.   5.

One survivor was Eva Hart. She and her parents have originally planned to travel on another
                                                               6.
ship, but the workers of that ship went on strike. The Harts were transferred to the *Titanic*. While
                                                                                                  7.
they were get on the ship, Mrs. Hart was afraid, but seven-year-old Eva was excited about the trip.
     8.
She had never even seeing a ship before, and now she was going to travel on the most luxurious ship
        9.
that has ever been built.
         10.

     While Eva was sleeping, her parents were hearing a noise. Mr. Hart went up to see what
     11.   12.
had happened. He returned to their cabin and had taken Eva and her mother to the top deck. He
     13.   14.
was put them on a lifeboat and said to Eva, "Hold onto Mummy's hand and be good." That was the
     15.   16.
last time she has seen her father. While they were on the lifeboat, they heard people screaming. Then
                17.   18.
suddenly everything had become quiet. The ship has gone down with her father and many others.
                         19.   20.
When they arrived in New York, her mother had decide to return to England. Eva has died in 1996 at
                                                       21.   22.
the age of 91.

     The last American survivor, Lillian Asplund, was just five years old when she traveling on
                                                                                       23.
the ship with her parents and brothers. They were returning to the U.S. from Sweden, where they
                                                24.
had spent several years. While they went to the top deck, she and her mother got on a lifeboat with
     25.   26.   27.
one of her brothers, but her father and other three brothers have waited for the next lifeboat. She
                                                               28.
never saw her father and brothers again. Lillian has died in 2006, at the age of ninety-nine. She was
     29.   30.
the last person with a memory of the tragedy. Another person, Millvina Dean, was the last survivor,

but she was a baby at the time so she hasn't remembered anything.
                                       31.
     I recently came across Jack Thayer's diary. For the past few weeks, I am reading it. It's an
                                                                           32.
amazing account of his experiences.

PART 3 Write About It

1. Find two articles about exploration or transportation. They can be articles about land, air, space, or sea. Or they can be about an explorer or inventor. Read the two articles and summarize them. Use your own words in the summary. Attach the articles to your summary.

2. Write about a trip you took where there were some difficulties to overcome.

PART 4 Edit Your Writing

Reread the Summary of Lesson 4 and the editing advice. Edit your writing from Part 3.

5

Modals and Related Expressions

Scientists study computer-generated
3-D simulations of nuclear reactions.

TECHNOLOGY

> The real danger is not that computers will begin to think like men, but that men will begin to think like computers.
>
> — Sydney J. Harris

PASSWORDS, PASSWORDS, **PASSWORDS**

Digital image of a lock created on a computer system board

PASSWORDS PASSWORDS

🎧 **Read the following article. Pay special attention to the words in bold.**

CD 1
TR 26

Technology **is supposed to make** our lives easier, but it can also be frustrating at times. You **may be** overwhelmed by the number of passwords you **have to have**: for your bank account, shopping sites, airlines, social media, e-mail, and so on. You **have got to remember** which password goes with which account. Each account has special requirements for passwords. For some accounts, you **must include** at least one uppercase[1] letter. For other accounts, you **have to include** at least one number. In some cases your password **must be** at least eight characters long and include a number and an uppercase letter. To prevent identity theft, experts say you **should change** your password at least once a month. You **might ask** yourself, "How **can** anyone **keep** track of[2] so many passwords?"

If you forget your password, you **can** usually **retrieve**[3] it by clicking on "forgot password." You sometimes **have to answer** security questions that you answered when you opened your account. For example, you **might be asked**, "What is your mother's maiden name?" or "In what city was your father born?" But the answers to some security questions are not so easy. For example, the answer to "Who is your favorite athlete?" **could change** over time. Even a simple question like "What school did you go to when you were ten years old?" **might have** several answers. The correct answer **could be** "Taft," or "Taft Elementary School." Your answer **has to match** the original one exactly.

Sometimes technology can be frustrating, but most people today would rather not live without it.

---

[1] *uppercase:* in capital letters
[2] *to keep track of:* to pay close attention to something
[3] *to retrieve:* to get something back

COMPREHENSION CHECK Based on the reading, tell if the statement is true (**T**) or false (**F**).

1. It's a good idea to change your password every month.

2. It's possible to use the same password for most of your accounts.

3. All passwords require an uppercase letter or a number.

5.1 Modals — An Overview

The modal verbs are *can, could, should, would, may, might,* and *must.* Modals add meaning to the verbs that follow them.

Examples	Explanation
You **should change** your password frequently. The password for my bank account **must include** at least one number.	A base form follows a modal. A modal never has an *-s* ending.
You **should not** tell anyone your password. I **cannot** remember so many passwords.	To form the negative, we put *not* after the modal. The negative of *can* is written as one word: *cannot.* The contraction for *cannot* is *can't.*
Passwords **should be changed** frequently. Passwords **must be entered** exactly.	To form the passive with a modal, we use the modal + *be* + past participle.
I **can't remember** so many passwords. = I **am not able to remember** so many passwords. You **must use** letters and numbers. = You **have to use** letters and numbers.	Expressions that are like modals in meaning are: *have to, have got to, be able to, be allowed to, be permitted to, be supposed to, had better.*

Observe these seven patterns with a modal:

AFFIRMATIVE STATEMENT:	You **should choose** a password.
NEGATIVE STATEMENT:	You **shouldn't choose** your name or birthday.
YES/NO QUESTION:	**Should** you **choose** a long password?
SHORT ANSWER:	Yes, you **should.**
WH- QUESTION:	Why **should** you **choose** a long password?
NEGATIVE *WH-* QUESTION:	Why **shouldn't** you **choose** your name?
SUBJECT QUESTION:	Who **should choose** a long password?

EXERCISE 1 Listen to this conversation and fill in the blanks with the words you hear.

CD 1
TR 27

A: I'm trying to get into my credit card account, but I ___can't remember___ my password.
                                                                       1.

B: It's so frustrating. I _____ my passwords, either. I _____ them
                              2.   3.

down. Otherwise I _____ them. The problem is I
                    4.

_____ where I put the paper.
5.

A: I was told that you _____ them down. What if someone _____ into
                          6.   7.

all your accounts?

continued

Modals and Related Expressions **135**

B: Well, most sites have a "forgot your password" link.

A: The problem is, they often tell me I _____ 8. a completely new password.

They sometimes say, "You _____ 9. a password that you haven't used in the past

year." So then I _____ 10. of something completely new—and remember it!

B: Another frustration is this: if I'm doing online banking and I leave the computer for ten minutes, I get

timed out. Then I _____ 11. all over again.

A: I thought technology _____ 12. our lives easier.

B: It _____ 13. our lives in some ways, but in other ways, it has made our lives more

complicated.

5.2 Possibility: *May, Might, Could*

Examples	Explanation
The answer to my security question **might** be "King" or it **may** be "King High School" or it **could** be "King HS." I don't remember.	We use *may, might,* or *could* to show possibility about the present.
I **may** open a new account. I **might** start to do my banking online.	We use *may* or *might* to show possibility about the future.
You **may not** remember all your passwords. You **might not** be happy with technology.	For negative possibility, we use *may not* or *might not.* We don't make a contraction with *may not* or *might not.*
Maybe my password is my dog's name. My password **may be** my dog's name.	*Maybe,* written as one word, is an adverb. It usually comes before the subject. *May be,* written as two words, is a modal + verb. It comes after the subject.
I **may/might** change my password. **Maybe** I will change my password.	Compare using the modals *may* or *might* for the future with using *maybe* for the future.

Language Note:

We don't use *could not* for negative possibility. It means *was/were not able to.*

EXERCISE 2 This is a conversation between a granddaughter and a grandfather about technology. Change the *maybe* statement under each blank to a statement using the modal given.

A: _____*I might buy*_____ a new computer. If I do, Grandpa, do you want my old one? It's two years old.
  1. maybe I'll buy/might

B: _____ two years old is old, but for me it's practically new. The one I have now is
  2. maybe you think/may

good enough for me. I just do e-mail.

A: There's more than e-mail on a computer. _____ to try social media.
  3. maybe you'll want/may

B: I'm not interested in those things. _____ a lot of online friends, but I'd rather
          4. maybe you have/may

   have two or three very good friends.

A: OK. But there are practical things you can do too. Have you ever tried online banking?

   _____ easier for you.
     5. maybe it will be/might

B: _____ right. But I like going into my bank and talking to real people.
       6. maybe you are/could

A: Why don't you just try it? Let me show you how.

B: No, thanks. I'll have to get a password. And _____ it.
                                                  7. maybe I won't remember/may

A: If you think you'll forget it, you can keep a record of your passwords, using hints.

B: What do you mean?

A: For example, if my password is my dog's name, my hint is "DOG." Let me help you get a hint for each password.

B: If I tell you my passwords, _____ all my money!
                                   8. maybe you will steal/might

A: Very funny, Grandpa.

5.3 Necessity/Obligation: *Must, Have To, Have Got To*

Examples	Explanation
This password **must** include one uppercase letter. It **must** be at least eight characters long.	*Must* shows necessity or obligation based on a rule, a law, or an instruction. It has an official or formal tone.
Sometimes you **have to** answer security questions. Your password **has to** have at least one number.	*Have to* shows necessity or obligation. It has a less official tone than *must*.
For my bank account, I**'ve got to** choose a password. It**'s got to** be very strong.	*Have got to* is an informal way to show necessity or obligation. *Have* and *has* are usually contracted with the subject pronoun.
My old computer was too slow. I **had to** buy a new one last week.	For past necessity or obligation, we use *had to*.

Language Notes:

1. Avoid using *must* for personal obligations. It sounds very official or urgent and is too strong
   for personal situations. Use *have to* or *have got to*.
     I **have to** open an online account.
     I**'ve got to** choose a username and password.

2. When using *have to*, don't make a contraction with the subject pronoun and *have*.

Pronunciation Notes:

1. *Have to* is usually pronounced /hæftə/.

2. *Has to* is usually pronounced /hæstə/.

3. With *have got to, have* is often dropped in informal speech. *Has* is not dropped. In informal
   writing, *got to* is sometimes written as "gotta."

EXERCISE 3 Two friends are talking about online banking. Use the phrases from the box to fill in the blanks. Use contractions where possible.

have got to meet	must use	have to do	have to fill out	must have
have to remember	have to click	have got to leave ✓	have to log on	has got to match
have got to copy	have got to include	must be copied	had to learn	

A: Can you help me access my bank account online?

B: I <u>'ve got to leave</u> in about 15 minutes. But I think we have enough time. First you
       1.

_____. Have you ever signed in before?
       2.

A: I'm not sure. Maybe not.

B: Then you _____ "register here."
       3.

A: OK. Now I _____ this long form.
       4.

B: The information here _____ the information on your bank account. So if you
       5.

used "David," you _____ "David" here, too. Don't use "Dave."
       6.

A: Of course, I knew that!

B: Now you need a password. It _____ at least one uppercase letter. And you
       7.

_____ at least one number.
       8.

A: OK. But now I'm going to _____ one more password. Now what do I
       9.

_____?
       10.

B: See those funny letters and numbers? You _____ them.
       11.

A: They're so hard to read. What's this for?

B: It's a safety feature. The letters and numbers _____ exactly.
       12.

A: You're so good with computers.

B: I haven't always been so good. I _____
       13.

just like you. It's getting late, and I _____
       14.

a friend in half an hour.

A: Thanks for your help! See you later.

Enter the following:

New Words

freezing temps

Vision Impaired

Help

Your Answer:

Continue

CAPTCHA

EXERCISE 4 [About You] Write a few obligations you have at your job, at your school, with your friends, or with your family. Use modals of necessity or obligation. Share your answers with a partner.

1. <u>My grandmother bought a new computer. I have to help her set it up on Saturday.</u>

2. _____

3. _____

4. _____

5. _____

5.4 Expectation: *Be Supposed To*

Be supposed to is used to express an expectation.

Examples	Explanation
I'm supposed to help my grandfather with his computer. **I'm supposed to** use at least one uppercase letter in my password. Technology **is supposed to** make our lives simpler, but sometimes it doesn't.	Something may be expected because of: • a personal obligation • a law or a requirement • something we are told to expect
I know **I'm supposed to** change my password every month, but I don't do it. I know **I'm not supposed to** write down my passwords, but I do.	*Be supposed to* shows a rule that is frequently broken or an expectation that isn't met.
I **was supposed to** help you with your computer yesterday, but I forgot.	For the past, we use *was/were supposed to*. It shows an expectation or obligation that was not met.

Pronunciation Note:

The *d* in *supposed to* is not pronounced.

EXERCISE 5 Fill in the blanks using a form of *be supposed to* and one of the words from the box. If you see *not,* use the negative form. Use contractions where possible.

pay	read✓	text	make	simplify	meet
send	copy	memorize	help	open	use

1. When you see "I accept," you <u>'re supposed to read</u> what it says, but most people don't.

2. Typing those funny letters and numbers _____ the website safer.

3. You _____ those numbers and letters exactly as you see them.

continued

4. My friends and I share music online. I know we _____ for the music, but we often

give it to each other for free.

5. I know I _____ all my passwords, but I can't. So I write them in a notebook.

6. Students (*not*) _____ in class, but I often see them texting under their desks.

7. My bank _____ me a statement each month, but I didn't get one this month.

I'll look for it online.

8. I typed in my password, but I got an error message. Oh, now I know what I did wrong.

I _____ uppercase for the first letter, but I used lowercase by mistake.

9. Children under 13 (*not*) _____ a social media account, but some kids lie about

their age and open an account anyway.

10. My grandparents don't know much about computers. I _____ them this weekend.

11. You _____ me at 6:00 to help me with my computer. It's 7:30. Did you forget?

EXERCISE 6 Report some rules in the following places: in your home or dorm, in traffic, on
the Internet, in a library, in class, on an airplane, or at an airport. Use *must* to give an official tone.
Use *have to* or *be supposed to* to give an informal tone.

1. In an airport, you must take off your shoes when you go through security.

2. In my dorm, we're not supposed to make noise after 11 p.m.

3. _____

4. _____

5. _____

EXERCISE 7 About You Write some rules, customs, or expectations that you don't (or didn't)
follow. Discuss your answers with a partner.

1. I'm supposed to turn off my cell phone in class, but I sometimes forget to do it.

2. I was supposed to write a paper for my history class, but I didn't have time.

3. _____

4. _____

5. _____

5.5 Advice: *Should, Ought To, Had Better*

Examples	Explanation
You **should** change your password every month. You **shouldn't** use your birthday.	*Should* shows advisability. It is used to say that something is a good idea. *Shouldn't* means that something is a bad idea.
Before I click "accept," I **ought to** read the terms, but I never do. You **ought to** use online banking. It's much quicker than going into a bank.	*Ought to* is another way of saying *should*. It is usually pronounced like one word: "oughta." It is the only modal followed by *to*. *Ought to* is not usually used for negatives and questions.
My password is too weak. I**'d better** choose a stronger one. Your password should be a secret. You**'d better not** tell it to anyone.	*Had better* is used in conversation and informal writing for advisability. It states or implies a negative consequence. We use **'d** to contract *had* with a pronoun.

Language Note:

In speech, the **'d** in *had better* is often omitted completely.

> You **better** not tell your password to anyone.

EXERCISE 8 Give advice for each situation. Practice *should, ought to,* and *had better.*

1. My computer is about seven years old. It's very slow.

   In my opinion, you should throw it away and buy a new one. A seven-year-old computer
   is too old.

2. I can't decide if I should buy a laptop or a desktop computer.

   _____

   _____

3. My little brother uses my laptop a lot. I think it now has a virus.

   _____

   _____

4. My daughter is ten years old and wants a social media account.

   _____

   _____

5. I have at least twenty-five passwords, and I can't remember them. So I wrote them all down and keep the paper near my computer.

   _____

   _____

EXERCISE 9 Fill in the blanks with one of the phrases from the box.

you shouldn't make	I should give	he shouldn't play	should I buy✓	I'd better do	you ought to protect	should I do
you'd better not use	you'd better be	you should choose	he ought to play	you ought to set up	'd better choose	

1. **A:** My old computer isn't fast enough. _____Should I buy_____ a new one or add more memory

   · to my old one? My computer's already nine years old.

   B: That's a *very* old computer.

   A: Maybe _____ it to my grandson.

   B: He probably likes to play games. So he's probably not interested in a slow computer.

   A: You're right. But I think _____ computer games.

   _____ with friends, not just computers.

2. **A:** Can I use your laptop for a few minutes? Can you fill in your password?

   B: I don't have a password.

   A: That's not good. _____ your laptop with a password.

   B: I don't think that's necessary. That's just one more password to remember.

   A: What if someone steals your laptop? _____ it easy for the thief to access

   your accounts. Mine was stolen in a coffee shop once.

   B: Really? How did that happen?

   A: I left it on the table and went to buy coffee. When I came back, it was gone!

   _____ careful and password protect your computer as soon as possible.

   B: _____ it right now. I'll use my birthday.

   A: _____ such an obvious password. Choose something that's more secure.

3. **A:** My younger brother uses my laptop when I'm at work. Sometimes he goes into my files. What

   _____?

   B: _____ a guest account. That way he can't get into your files.

A: How do I do that?

B: I can help you. Let me see your computer … OK. I set up a guest account for you. A guest doesn't need a password, but your account does. _____ a password that your

c.

brother can't guess.

A: Even more important, I _____ a password that I can remember!

d.

EXERCISE 10 Circle the correct modal or expression to complete the sentences. In some cases, both answers are possible. In those cases, circle both choices.

1. You (*'d better not*/*must not*) write your passwords on a piece of paper. What if someone finds the paper?

2. For each new account, you (*'ve got to*/*should*) choose a password.

3. Some websites require an uppercase letter. For those sites, you (*'re supposed to*/*ought to*) include at least one uppercase letter.

4. I'm so tired of passwords. Why (*do I have to*/*should I*) remember so many passwords?

5. Sometimes when you forget your password, you (*have to*/*'d better*) answer some questions, such as "What's the name of your pet?"

6. You (*must*/*should*) choose a password that's hard for other people to guess. So it's not a good idea to use your birthday.

7. I know I (*ought to*/*should*) create a strong password, but I like using the same password for all my accounts.

8. I got timed out of my account when I answered the phone. When I came back, I (*had to*/*must*) log in again.

9. Your password is case sensitive. That means you (*must*/*ought to*) type it exactly the way you typed it originally, with uppercase and lowercase letters.

10. They say you (*should*/*must*) change your password every month, but I never do.

11. My grandmother needs help with her online bank account. I promised to help her tomorrow. She

(*is supposed to*/*must*) bring her laptop to my house. But it (*must*/*is supposed to*) snow tomorrow, so I don't

a.   b.

know if she's still coming.

12. Those funny letters and numbers are so hard to read. You (*ought to*/*'ve got to*) copy them exactly.

EXERCISE 11 About You Write sentences about computers, passwords, online shopping, online banking, or online music using the words given. Discuss your sentences with a partner.

1. have to _____ *When I order something online, I have to pay for shipping.* _____

2. should _____

3. have got to _____

4. must _____

5. ought to _____

6. had better _____

7. be supposed to _____

5.6 Suggestion: *Can/Could*

Examples	Explanation
To remember passwords, you **can** create a hint for each password. You **could** keep the hint in a notebook.	We use *can* and *could* to give suggestions.
You **can** open a bank account online, or you **could** go into the bank and do it in person. You **should** change your password frequently.	We use *can* or *could* when several options are possible. We use *should* when you feel that there is only one right way.

EXERCISE 12 Offer two suggestions to answer each of the following questions. You may work with a partner. Use *can* or *could*.

1. How can I make my password more secure?

   You can mix uppercase and lowercase letters. You could include a number or symbol.

2. How can I open a new bank account?

   _____

3. How can I remember all my passwords?

   _____

4. How can I pay for something online?

   _____

5. How can I compare prices on a new TV?

   _____

Taking a Break from Technology

Subject   modal   verb/base
they   may not take
Campers   can   get

Read the following article. Pay special attention to the words in bold.

Levi Felix has started a new kind of summer camp in California called Camp Grounded. Even though it's only three days long, campers can get away from their daily routine and swim, hike, take yoga classes, and enjoy nature. Most of all, campers can interact with each other. So what's so special about this camp? It's only for adults. And there's one important rule: Campers **must not** be connected to technology while there.

Many adults report that when they are on vacation, they **aren't able to** stay away from their devices and often check their work-related e-mails. Even when out in nature, they **may not** take the time to admire a spectacular mountain before pulling out their smartphone to take a picture.

Levi Felix wants people to interact with each other, not with their tech devices. At Camp Grounded, campers **are not allowed to** talk about their jobs. They **are not** even **permitted to** use their real names.

They have to pick a nickname. They are supposed to get to know each other as people, not through their professional lives. Felix hopes that campers can get to know themselves better as well.

Why do people have to go to camp to do this? Why not just unplug for the weekend? Many people say that they **can't** control themselves when they have a device nearby. They know they **don't have to** respond every time they hear a beep from their phone, but they do.

Felix is not against technology, but he thinks technology **shouldn't** control us. We **don't have to** give up our devices, but we need more balance in our lives.

A young woman practices yoga at a mountain lake.

COMPREHENSION CHECK Based on the reading, tell if the statement is true (**T**) or false (**F**).

1. Levi Felix has created a technology camp for adults.

2. At Felix's camp, people talk about their professions.

3. Felix wants adults to interact with each other at his camp.

5.7 Negative Modals

Examples	Explanation
Campers **must not** be connected to technology while there.	*Must not* shows that something is prohibited. It has an official tone.
Campers **cannot** use technology at this camp. They **may not** talk about work. They **are not allowed to** use a cell phone. They **are not permitted to** use their real names.	*Cannot* and *may not* show that something is not permitted. The meaning is similar to *must not* but is less formal. Other expressions that show prohibition are *be not allowed to* and *be not permitted to*.
Campers **are not supposed to** talk about their jobs. I **wasn't supposed to** use my cell phone at camp, but I did.	*Be not supposed to* is also used to show that something is not permitted. It is often used when a rule has already been broken.
Technology **shouldn't** control you. You should control technology.	*Should not* shows that something is not advisable.
If your phone beeps, you **don't have to** respond to it immediately. You can wait.	*Not have to* shows that something is not necessary or required.

Language Notes:

1. In the affirmative, *have to* and *must* have the same meaning, although *must* sounds more official.

    You **must** give up your cell phone for three days. = You **have to** give up your cell phone for three days.

2. In the negative, the meanings are completely different. *Must not* shows prohibition. *Not have to* shows that something is not necessary or required.

    One camp rule is that you **must not** use a cell phone for three days.

    When my cell phone rings, I **don't have to** answer it. I can wait.

EXERCISE 13 Circle the correct words in each item. In some cases, both answers are possible. In those cases, circle both choices.

1. At Camp Grounded, you (*may not*/*don't have to*) use a cell phone.

2. When your phone rings, you (*cannot*/*don't have to*) answer it if it's not an emergency.

3. According to Levi Felix, technology (*shouldn't*/*can't*) control you.

4. At Camp Grounded, you (*don't have to*/*are not allowed to*) use technology.

5. Campers (*aren't supposed to*/*don't have to*) bring their devices to camp, but some of them do.

6. According to the camp rules, you (*must not*/*may not*) use a tech device for three days.

7. If you don't want to take a yoga class at camp, you (*must not*/*don't have to*). It's your choice.

8. I want a break from technology. I (*don't have to*/*shouldn't*) go to camp. I can just turn off my phone.

9. You (*may not*/*don't have to*) use a computer at Camp Grounded.

EXERCISE 14 Circle the correct words to complete the conversation. In some cases, both answers are possible. In those cases, circle both choices.

A: Every time I get a credit card or bank statement, I just throw it in the garbage.

B: You (*shouldn't*/*don't have to*) do that. Someone (*can*/*should*) steal your identity. I read that thieves go
           1.   2.

through the garbage looking for personal information.

A: But they (*don't have to*/*can't*) use my number without my credit card.
                         3.

B: They can and they do. They make purchases by phone and charge it to your credit card. You

(*may not*/*might not*) realize your information has been stolen till you review your bill a month later.
   4.

You (*must not*/*shouldn't*) just throw away papers with personal information. You (*must*/*should*) shred
     5.   6.

them. You (*could*/*can*) buy a shredder at an office supply store or online. Look. On this shopping site,
     7.

if you spend over $25, you (*are not supposed to*/*don't have to*) pay for shipping.
                         8.

A: OK. I'll buy one.

B: I do all my bill payments online. This way I (*don't have to*/*must not*) write any checks.
                                       9.

A: I don't know how to set up an online account. Can you help me?

B: Sure. Let's find your bank's website. OK. Now choose a password. You (*shouldn't*/*don't have to*) use
                                                   10.

your birthday. It's too easy for a thief to figure out.

A: OK. Let me try my mother's maiden name. Oh. It rejected this.

B: You used all letters. You (*couldn't*/*can't*) use just letters. You (*have to*/*can*) include at least one number.
                              11.   12.

Now try to memorize it.

A: I (*'m not supposed to*/*can't*) memorize so many passwords. It's impossible.
     13.

B: You (*have to*/*'ve got to*) find a way to keep track of your passwords.
     14.

EXERCISE 15 About You Write about a rule, law, or custom from your country or culture that other people may find strange.

1. In Rwanda, children are supposed to greet older people. _____

2. _____

USING TECHNOLOGY to ENFORCE the LAW

CD 1
TR 29

🎧 **Read the following article. Pay special attention to the words in bold.**

Michelle O'Brien of Chicago opened her mail one day and found a surprise—but not a pleasant surprise. It was a traffic ticket for going through a red light two weeks earlier. Ms. O'Brien had always thought of herself as a careful driver and thought, "This **must** be a mistake. I always stop at a red light." But the evidence was unmistakable: the city sent her a link to a website, where she **could** clearly see her car in the intersection after the light had turned red.

Welcome to the world of photo-enforced intersections. Many cities in the United States and Canada have been using photo-enforced red lights at busy intersections for several years. Chicago now has about two hundred of them. We all know we're not supposed to go through a red light. But sometimes we don't even realize that we're doing it.

How do cities choose where to put a camera? City officials study the intersections that have the most serious accidents. While the number of serious side collisions goes down at these places, often there are more rear-end collisions. When a driver stops suddenly for a red light, the driver behind him sometimes **can't** stop in time.

Many drivers think that this kind of technology is a nuisance.[4] They say this is just a way for the city or state to collect more money. Others say the government **shouldn't** have so much information about us. But photo-enforced red lights **could** save lives.

---

[4] *nuisance:* a bother; something that causes irritation or frustration

A traffic-monitoring camera

COMPREHENSION CHECK Based on the reading, tell if the statement is true (**T**) or false (**F**).

1. The United States is the only country that has photo-enforced red lights.

2. You can get a ticket in the mail.

3. Photo-enforced red lights reduce the number of rear-end collisions.

5.8 Ability/Possibility: *Can, Be Able To*

Examples	Explanation
The light is turning yellow. I think you **can** stop. If the street is wet, you **can't** stop quickly.	*Can* shows ability or possibility.
Are you **able to** see the camera at the red light?	*Be able to* is another way to express ability/possibility.
Could you stop? = **Were** you **able to** stop? I **couldn't** stop. = I **wasn't able to** stop.	We use *could* or *was/were able to* for past questions and negative statements.
I **was able to** stop when the light turned yellow. I **could** drive for many hours without stopping when I was younger.	In affirmative past statements, we use *was/were able to* for a single past action. We use *could* to express *used to be able to*.

Pronunciation Note:

Can is not usually stressed in affirmative statements. In negative statements, *can't* is stressed, but it is hard to hear the final ***t***. We must pay attention to the stress to hear the difference between *can* and *can't*.

    I can gó. /kɪn/   I cán't go. /kænt/

EXERCISE 16 There are many ways drivers can be distracted. Fill in the blanks with one of the phrases from the box to complete the statements about driver distraction.

can eat	can't do	are you able to keep	are able to read	can do ✓
can change	are able to reach	can look at	can talk	couldn't answer

1. Some drivers think they _____ *can do* _____ other things safely while driving. But driver distraction is dangerous.

2. _____ your eyes on the road and text at the same time? Absolutely not.

3. Most drivers know that it's dangerous to send a text message while driving. But some drivers think they _____ a text message while driving.

4. You probably think you _____ the station on your radio without being distracted, but even this can be dangerous.

5. Some drivers think they _____ a sandwich or drink a cup of coffee while driving.

continued

6. Some drivers think they _____ for something in the back seat, but this can be

   dangerous, too.

7. You might think you _____ while driving, but even conversations cause a distraction.

8. If there's an accident on the road, we think we _____ what's happening

   without taking our eyes off the road. But this can be dangerous.

9. My phone rang while I was driving. But I _____ it at that time.

5.9 Logical Conclusion: *Must*

Examples	Explanation
When Michelle saw the ticket, she thought, "This **must** be a mistake. I'm always such a careful driver." I hear you're going to a no-tech camp. It **must** be hard to give up your devices for a few days.	*Must* shows that something is probably true. It is used to make a conclusion based on information we have or observations we make.
How many passwords do you have? I **must** have at least fifty.	We can use *must* to make an estimate.
A: My brother always speeds up when he approaches a yellow light. **B:** He **must not** know about photo-enforced lights. **A:** He knows. **B:** Then he **must not** be a very good driver.	For a negative conclusion, we use *must not*. We don't use a contraction.

EXERCISE 17   Use context clues and fill in the blanks with an appropriate verb to make a logical conclusion. Answers will vary.

1. **A:** I signed up for a no-tech camp. I plan on having a vacation from technology.

   B: You must ___*feel*___ nervous about being without your devices for a few days.

　　　　　　　 a.

   A: I'm not nervous. I'm looking forward to a break from technology.

2. **A:** Kids love technology. They don't want to be without it for a minute.

   B: Teachers must ___*feel (be)*___ angry when cell phones ring during class.

　　　　　　　　 a.

   A: The kids are smart about it. They silence their phones in class.

3. **A:** I have a computer problem. I don't know how to fix it.

   B: Ask your teenage son. He's on his computer all day. He must ___*know*___ what to do. Kids

　　　　　　　　　　　　　　　　　　　　　　　　　　　　 a.

   know much more about computers than we do.

4. **A:** How many text messages do you send every day?

   B: A lot. I must _____send (write)_____ between 100 and 200 messages a day.
   a.

   A: You must not ~~have (be)~~ _____ using the telephone very much.
   b.

   B: For me, texting is more convenient than talking on the phone.

5. **A:** Do you use the same password for all your accounts?

   B: Of course not. Like most people, I must ~~have~~ _use_ more than 30 passwords.
   a.

   A: It must _____be_____ hard to remember so many passwords.
   b.

   B: It is. It's very hard.

6. **A:** Katya always sends and receives text messages during class.

   B: Who's Katya?

   A: You must _____know_____ who I'm talking about. She's the tall woman who sits between us
   a.

   in class.

   B: Oh, now I know. I always call her Kathy.

7. **A:** I hear your ringtone is a Beyoncé song.

   B: It is.

   A: You must ~~listen~~ _like_ Beyoncé very much.
   a.

   B: I do. She's one of my favorite singers.

8. **A:** My brother got a ticket for not stopping at a red light.

   B: He must _____be_____ a bad driver. He must not _____have_____ much experience.
   a.   b.

   A: Not true. He's been driving for four years. He's actually a good driver. But when the light turns

   yellow, he speeds up.

   B: In my opinion, he's not a good driver.

9. **A:** Whenever I text my daughter, she usually writes "LOL." She probably means "Lots of love."

   B: You must not ~~understand~~ _know_ much about texting abbreviations. "LOL" means "laughing
   a.

   out loud."

Handwritten margin note: Negative + modal not with modal if positive has

5.10 Probability vs. Possibility: *Must* vs. *May, Might, Could*

Examples	Explanation
A: You've been driving for three hours. Let me drive now. You **must** be tired. **B:** You're right. I'm very tired. **A:** The city **must** make a lot of money from traffic tickets. **B:** This **must** mean that a lot of drivers are not obeying the law.	If something is probable because an observation leads to a logical conclusion, we use *must*. You **must** be tired. = You are probably tired. The city **must** make a lot of money. = The city probably makes a lot of money.
A: You **might** not realize it, but you just went through a red light. **B:** I'm sure it was yellow. **A:** You **may** think it was yellow, but you entered the intersection after the light turned red. **B:** I suppose you **could** be right. I hope there are no cameras here.	If something is possible but we don't have evidence to reach a conclusion, we use *may, might,* or *could*. These modals mean "maybe." You **might** not realize it. = Maybe you don't realize it. You **may** think it was yellow. = Maybe you think it was yellow.

EXERCISE 18 Did you ever notice that some drivers want to say something about themselves on their license plates? They pay extra money for these "vanity" plates. Here are some vanity plates. Work with a partner to make a statement about the owner of the car. If you and your partner agree on the owner's message, you have probably come to a logical conclusion and can use *must*. If you don't agree, the vanity message is not certain. Use *may, might,* or *could*.

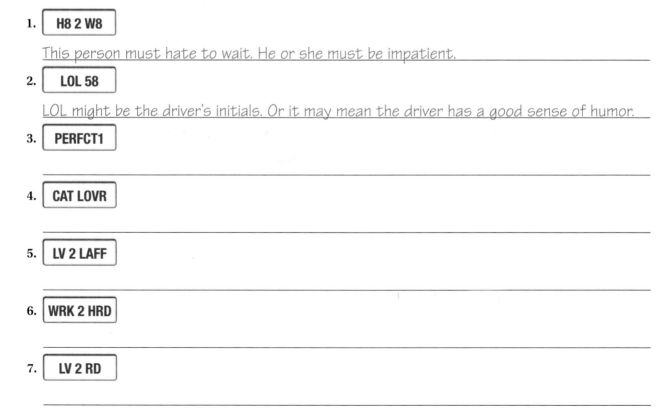

1. **H8 2 W8**

    This person must hate to wait. He or she must be impatient.

2. **LOL 58**

    LOL might be the driver's initials. Or it may mean the driver has a good sense of humor.

3. **PERFCT1**

4. **CAT LOVR**

5. **LV 2 LAFF**

6. **WRK 2 HRD**

7. **LV 2 RD**

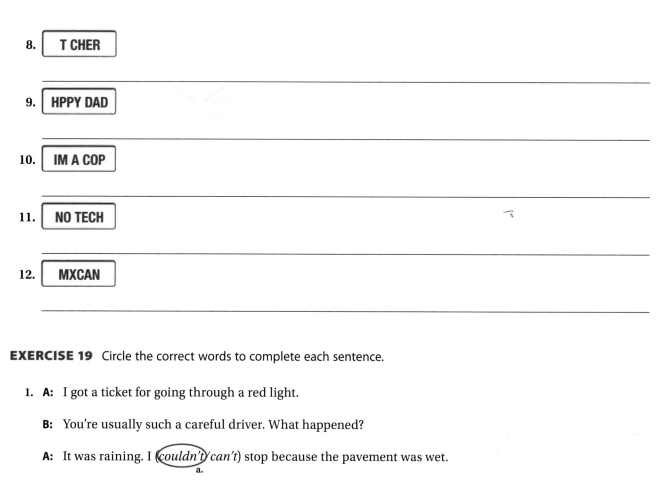

8. | T CHER |

9. | HPPY DAD |

10. | IM A COP |

11. | NO TECH |

12. | MXCAN |

EXERCISE 19 Circle the correct words to complete each sentence.

1. **A:** I got a ticket for going through a red light.

    B: You're usually such a careful driver. What happened?

    A: It was raining. I (*couldn't*/*can't*) stop because the pavement was wet.
      a.

    B: How much (*should you*/*do you have to*) pay?
      b.

    A: $100.

    B: You (*must*/*are supposed to*) be upset about that.
      c.

2. **A:** You didn't come to class yesterday. Were you sick?

    B: No, I wasn't. I (*couldn't*/*can't*) come to class because I (*had to*/*must*) go to traffic court.
      a.   b.

    A: I'll tell you the assignment. For next week, we (*should*/*'ve got to*) write a composition.
      c.

    We (*'re supposed to*/*'re able to*) write about how technology helps us in our daily lives.
      d.

3. **A:** Technology (*must*/*is supposed to*) make our lives easier. But I have so many passwords, and now I
      a.

    (*can't*/*don't have to*) remember all of them. I (*may*/*must*) have at least 25.
      b.   c.

    B: You (*should*/*must*) give yourself a hint for each one. For example, I have the hint "FRST SCHL."
      d.

    A: That's easy. It (*should*/*must*) mean "first school." What if someone (*is able to*/*is supposed to*)
      e.   f.

    understand your hint? Your friends (*might*/*are supposed to*) know it.
      g.

    B: I'm not worried about my friends. I'm worried about thieves!

    continued

4. **A:** I just filled out this online application. I clicked "I accept."

   B: You (*were supposed to/had to*) read the agreement before accepting.

a.

   A: Nobody reads that.

5. **A:** Did you read about Camp Grounded?

   B: It's not for me. I (*don't have to/can't*) be without my cell phone for a whole weekend.

a.

   A: You (*must/should*) be very dependent on it.

b.

   B: I am.

6. **A:** I'm so happy. My vacation starts tomorrow. I (*must not/don't have to*) work for a week. I hope I won't

a.

   be bored. Any ideas on what I can do?

   B: You (*must/could*) read. Or you (*can/should*) just surf the Internet.

b.　　　　　　　　　　c.

   A: I (*must/could*) spend at least twenty hours a week on my computer at work. Now that I'm on vacation,

d.

   I want a break from technology.

7. **A:** Can you help me with my computer problem this afternoon?

   B: Sorry, I can't. I (*'m supposed to/could*) help my mom this afternoon. She's expecting me.

a.

8. **A:** There are a lot of new photo-enforced red lights.

   B: We (*'d better/might*) be more careful or we could get a ticket.

a.

   A: Camera or no camera, we (*may/should*) always be careful.

b.

9. **A:** I heard your parents gave you $1,000 for your graduation. What are you going to do with the money?

   B: I (*might/must*) buy a new computer. I (*don't have to/must not*) make up my mind right away.

a.　　　　　　　　　　　　　　　　　　　b.

   I'm going to think about it first.

5.11 Continuous Modals

Examples	Explanation
My son is at camp. I haven't heard from him all week. He **must be having** a good time. Sam is looking at his phone under his desk. He **might be texting**. Or he **could be using** the Internet. He **should be paying** attention.	We use the modal + *be* + present participle (verb *-ing*) for a present continuous meaning.

EXERCISE 20 Fill in the blanks with a verb phrase from the box.

could be charging	should be slowing down	must be making
shouldn't be texting	might be taking ✓	should be reading
might be preventing	shouldn't be using	must be talking

1. **A:** My friend isn't answering his phone. I know he always has his cell phone with him.

   B: He _might be taking_ a shower now. I'm sure he doesn't take his phone into the shower!

   a.

   Or he _____ it now. Maybe his battery is dead.

   b.

2. **A:** I don't like photo-enforced red lights. The city _____ a lot of money that way.

   a.

   B: But the city _____ accidents, and that's a good thing.

   b.

3. **A:** You _____ in class.

   a.

   B: I know. But I have to send an important message to my mom right now.

4. **A:** Look at that driver. The light is turning yellow, and she's speeding up.

   B: That's dangerous. She _____ .

   a.

5. **A:** It looks like that man is talking to himself.

   B: He _____ on a cell phone. Look carefully. He's wearing headphones.

   a.

6. **A:** Hi. I'm at camp and I just wanted to say hello to you.

   B: You _____ your cell phone. You're at a no-tech camp! Follow the rules.

   a.

7. **A:** For this account, I'm supposed to click "I accept." I know I _____ all this,

   a.

   but it's long.

   B: You're like most people. Nobody wants to read all that.

SUMMARY OF LESSON 5

Examples	Meaning
Cars **must** have a license plate. A driver **must not** go through a red light.	Necessity or obligation because of a rule, law, or instruction (official tone) Negative: prohibition
I **have to** choose a password to bank online. She**'s got to** pay her traffic ticket. If your phone beeps, you **don't have to** look at it.	Necessity or obligation (unofficial tone) Negative: not necessary
I**'m supposed to** read the agreement before clicking "I accept." But I never do. Technology **is supposed to** make our lives easier. At a no-tech camp, campers **are not supposed to** bring their cell phones, but some people do.	Expectation because of a rule or requirement, or because we are told what to expect Negative: prohibition; rule often broken or instructions not followed
You **should** change your password frequently. You **ought to** use a combination of lowercase and uppercase letters. You **shouldn't** use your name or birthday in your password.	Advisability Negative: not advisable
You look sleepy. You**'d better** let me drive for a while. You**'d better not** drive anymore.	Warning: negative consequence is stated or implied
You **can/may** choose your own license plate number. You **are allowed to/are permitted to** continue if the light turns yellow. You **can't/may not** park here. We **are not permitted to/are not allowed to** text in class.	Permission Negative: Prohibition; less formal than *must not*
My grandmother **can't** drive at night. Her night vision isn't good. When she was younger, she **could** drive with no problem at night.	Ability/Inability Past ability/Inability
If you enter the intersection after the light turns red, you **may/might/could** get a ticket in the mail.	Possibility
How **can** I get away from technology? You **could** turn off all your devices for a few days. Or you **can** go to a no-tech camp.	Suggestions
It **must** be hard for some people to give up technology for a few days. I **must** have at least fifty passwords.	Logical conclusion about the present An estimate

TEST / REVIEW

Each item mentions an aspect of enrolling for an online bank account. Circle the right words to complete the statement. In some cases, both answers are correct, so circle both options.

1. Enroll online or call this toll-free number: 800-555-1234

    I (*can*/*might*) enroll online, or I (*could*/*must*) call a toll-free number.
      a.   b.

2. If you call us, please have your Social Security number ready.

    I (*don't have to*/*can't*) apply for online banking without a Social Security number.
      a.

3. Choose a password. Use at least one uppercase letter, one lowercase letter, one symbol, and one number.

    I (*have*/*'ve got*) to choose a complicated password. How (*am I supposed to*/*must I*) remember all of that?
      a.   b.

4. Apply now. You can have an account in a few minutes.

    I (*must not*/*don't have to*) go into a bank. I (*can*/*should*) do my banking any time of day.
      a.   b.

5. We need a driver's license or state ID.

    I don't have a driver's license. It says I (*am supposed to*/*can*) use a state ID.
                                                     a.

6. What's the best phone number where we can reach you? What is your alternate number? (optional)

    I (*shouldn't*/*don't have to*) give an alternate phone number.
      a.

7. There are three types of accounts. Choose one.

    I'm not sure which is the best for me. I (*ought to*/*should*) call the bank for more information..
                                                    a.

8. After you read the agreement, click "I accept."

    I (*'m supposed to*/*may*) read the whole agreement, but it's too hard to understand.
      a.

9. For information in Spanish, click here. (Para información en español, haga clic aquí.)

    Spanish speakers (*should*/*can*) get information in Spanish.
                                   a.

10. Do you want to sign up for automatic bill payment? (Optional)

    I (*can*/*have to*) sign up for automatic bill payment if I want to.
      a.

11. There are so many questions on this application.

    There (*must*/*should*) be at least 30 questions. It (*could*/*was supposed to*) be an easy process, but it's not.
      a.   b.

12. If you apply today, you will get a check for $50.

    That's sounds like a good idea. I (*am supposed to*/*should*) apply today.
                                              a.

13. Only U.S. citizens can apply online. If you are not a U.S. citizen, please visit one of our banking locations.

    I (*must*/*have to*) be a U.S. citizen to apply online. I'm not a U.S. citizen, so I (*can't*/*must not*) apply online.
      a.   b.

WRITING

PART 1 Editing Advice

1. Don't use *to* after a modal (exception: *ought to*).

You should ~~to~~ drive more carefully.

2. Don't forget the *d* in *supposed to*.

You are suppose_∧to stop at a red light. *(d inserted)*

You are suppose ^d to stop at a red light.

3. Don't forget the *d* to express *had* in *had better*.

You ^'d better not talk on your cell phone while driving.

4. Use *have/has* before *got to*.

You ^'ve got to have a password for each account.

5. Don't forget *be* or *to* in these expressions: *be supposed to, be able to, be permitted to, be allowed to*.

You ^are supposed to have license plates on your car.

I'm not able ^to remember so many passwords.

6. Use correct word order in a question with a modal.

How ~~I can~~ *can I* get a vanity license plate?

7. Don't put *can* after another modal. Change to *be able to*.

You must ~~can~~ *be able to* drive well if you want to pass the driver's test.

PART 2 Editing Practice

Some of the shaded words and phrases have mistakes. Find the mistakes and correct them. If the shaded words are correct, write *C*.

I think technology isn't good for small children. Kids should ~~to~~ play with other kids, not just
1.

devices. How can they develop social skills if they always play with devices? I have a five-year-old
2. *C*

nephew. He must to spend at least four hours a day on his tablet. He doesn't even like to watch
3.

TV anymore. He should spend more time outdoors with other kids. I often tell my brother, "You
4.

better put some limits on how much time Kyle can play with his tablet." My brother always tells me,
5.

"What we can do? We're too busy to take him to the park to play." I think my brother and his wife
6.

supposed to set a good example for their son. Instead, Kyle sees his parents always texting, tweeting,
7.

checking e-mail, etc. They think he should be able have good technology skills before he goes to
8.

school. I can't convince my brother and sister-in-law to change their habits.
9.

My sister is raising her daughter differently. Maya is four years old, and she not permitted use
10.

technology at all. My sister thinks that Maya got to learn social skills first. She's not allow to watch
11.   12.

more than one TV program a day. In nice weather, she's got to play outside and get some exercise.
13.

Sometimes she sees her friends playing with a tablet. She asks my sister, "Why I can't have a tablet?"
14.

My sister has to explain to her that people are more important than electronic devices. It's not easy
15.

raising children today. But we got to set a good example for them.
16.

PART 3 Write About It

1. Write about some advantages and disadvantages of technology in our daily lives.

2. Do you think it's important to take a break from technology from time to time? Why or why not?

PART 4 Edit Your Writing

Reread the Summary of Lesson 5 and the editing advice. Edit your writing from Part 3.

The faces of U.S. presidents George Washington, Thomas Jefferson, Theodore Roosevelt, and Abraham Lincoln are carved into this granite mountain, Mount Rushmore, South Dakota.

U.S. PRESIDENTS
and ELECTIONS

> Those who deny freedom to others deserve it not for themselves.
>
> — Abraham Lincoln

LINCOLN and the GETTYSBURG ADDRESS

🎧 **Read the following article. Pay special attention to the words in bold.**

CD 1
TR 30

From the time of the first English colonies[1] in America, Africans were brought to America as slaves. Most of them were taken to the South, where they worked on farms in the production of sugar, cotton, and other crops.[2] White farmers in the South **couldn't have been** prosperous without slaves. But many Northerners were against slavery. One of those was Abraham Lincoln, the president who finally brought an end to slavery in the United States.

Today many people consider Abraham Lincoln to be one of the greatest presidents of the United States. But before he became president, many had doubts about his abilities. Lincoln's parents were poor and uneducated, and Lincoln had only eighteen months of schooling. But he loved to read, and he educated himself. Because Lincoln had so little schooling, journalists thought he **must not have been** very smart.

Much to his opponents' surprise, Lincoln won the presidential election in 1860. At that time, southern slave owners wanted to continue slavery, but Lincoln wanted to stop the spread of slavery. What followed was the worst internal crisis in American history: the Civil War. Over half a million soldiers died in the conflict, the most of any war that the United States fought in.

On November 19, 1863, President Lincoln was invited to say a few words at Gettysburg, Pennsylvania, where a terrible battle had taken place. There **must have been** about 20,000 people there. Edward Everett, the main speaker, spoke first. His speech lasted two hours. Lincoln followed Everett with a two-minute speech. When he finished, everyone was silent. The audience **may have been surprised** by the brevity[3] of the speech. Some people thought he **must not have been** finished. Seeing the reaction of the crowd, Lincoln turned to Everett and said he was afraid his speech had been a failure. He said he **should have prepared** it more carefully. Everett disagreed. He said the speech was perfect. He said the president had said more in two minutes than he, Everett, had said in two hours. This speech, known as the Gettysburg Address, is one of the greatest speeches in American history. Lincoln said that the country was dedicated to freedom and that "government of the people, by the people, for the people" had to continue.

The Civil War continued until April 9, 1865, when the North finally won. Less than a week later, Lincoln was assassinated.[4]

Illustration of Lincoln delivering his speech, in Gettysburg, Pennsylvania

---

[1] *colony:* a group of people who have moved to another area of land, but are still governed by their home country

[2] *crop:* plant grown as food, especially grains, vegetables, or fruit

[3] *brevity:* shortness

[4] *to assassinate:* to murder or kill

COMPREHENSION CHECK Based on the reading, tell if the statement is true (**T**) or false (**F**).

1. Lincoln didn't have much formal education.

2. Lincoln's short speech surprised the audience.

3. Lincoln was assassinated before the Civil War ended.

6.1 Modals in the Past — Form

Examples	Explanation
"I **should have prepared** the speech more carefully," thought Lincoln. Southern farmers **could not have become** rich without slaves.	To form the past of a modal, we use modal + (*not*) + *have* + past participle.
Lincoln probably **could have been elected** again, but he was assassinated. Africans **should not have been brought** to the U.S. to work as slaves.	To form the passive of a modal, we use modal + (*not*) + *have been* + past participle.

Pronunciation Note:

In informal speech, *have* is often pronounced like *of* or /ə/.

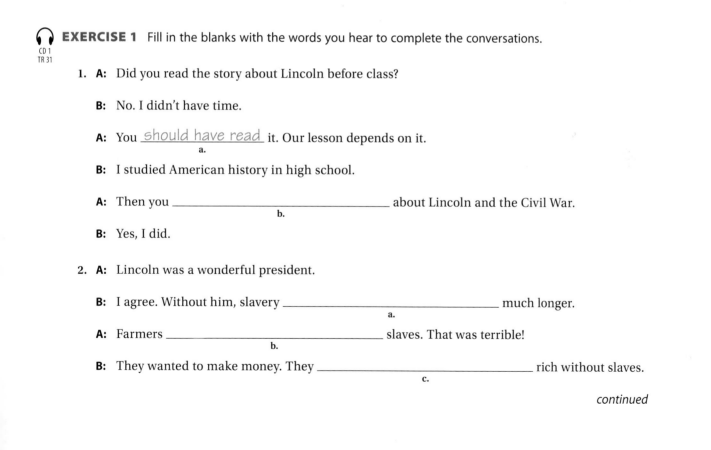

EXERCISE 1 Fill in the blanks with the words you hear to complete the conversations.

CD 1
TR 31

1. **A:** Did you read the story about Lincoln before class?

   B: No. I didn't have time.

   A: You <u>should have read</u> it. Our lesson depends on it.
   a.

   B: I studied American history in high school.

   A: Then you _____ about Lincoln and the Civil War.
   b.

   B: Yes, I did.

2. **A:** Lincoln was a wonderful president.

   B: I agree. Without him, slavery _____ much longer.
   a.

   A: Farmers _____ slaves. That was terrible!
   b.

   B: They wanted to make money. They _____ rich without slaves.
   c.

continued

3. **A:** Do you remember the story we read about Lewis and Clark?

   B: No. I _____ absent that day.

a.

   A: You weren't absent. And we talked about it for almost a week.

   B: Oh. Then I _____ much attention.

b.

   A: You _____ more attention in class. It was an interesting topic.

c.

4. **A:** Lincoln's speech was very short.

   B: He _____ it very fast.

a.

   A: I don't think he wrote it fast. I think he chose his words very carefully.

   B: Edward Everett's speech was two hours long. The audience _____ bored.

b.

   A: Maybe. I wouldn't like to listen to a two-hour speech.

5. **A:** I rented the movie *Lincoln,* but it was very hard for me to understand.

   B: You _____ subtitles.

a.

   A: I don't know how to do that.

   B: You _____ me. I do it all the time.

b.

6.2 Past Regrets or Mistakes — *Should Have*

Examples	Explanation
"**I should have given** a longer speech," thought Lincoln.	We use *should have* + past participle to comment on mistakes or regrets, or to rethink the advisability of a past decision.
I think Everett's speech was too long. He **shouldn't have talked** for such a long time.	We use *should not have* + past participle to say that a past action was not advisable.

EXERCISE 2 Fill in the blanks to express past advisability. Use context clues to help you.

1. **A:** There was a great documentary on TV about Lincoln last night. You should ___*have seen*___ it.

a.

   B: I didn't know about it. You should _____ me about it.

b.

   A: I did tell you. You sometimes write things in your calendar. You should

   _____ it down.

c.

2. **A:** I rented the movie *Lincoln*, and I thought it was boring. I only watched about twenty minutes of it.

   B: You should _____ the whole thing. It was very good.
                                a.

   A: I don't know much about American history. I never paid much attention to it in school.

   B: History's very important. You should _____ more attention.
                                                         b.

3. **A:** Did you vote in the last election? I know you're a U.S. citizen now.

   B: I forgot about it. But I really don't like what some politicians are doing now.

   A: Then you should _____. You're giving me your opinion now. You should
                                         a.

   _____ your opinion on election day too.
                   b.

4. **A:** I gave a long speech in my English class and everyone started to yawn. I should

   _____ it.
                   a.

   B: You're right. It's best to shorten a speech as much as possible.

   A: You should _____ me. You're good at giving speeches.
                                b.

   B: I didn't have time to help you. I had to prepare my own speech.

5. **A:** Slavery was a terrible thing. Farmers shouldn't _____ slaves to do their work.
                                                       a.

   B: I agree. It's an awful thing to use people that way.

   A: They should _____ workers to do the work.
                                b.

   B: They didn't want to pay workers. They wanted to make a lot of money for themselves.

6.3 Past Possibility — *May / Might / Could + Have*

Examples	Explanation

Why didn't the audience react after Lincoln's speech?
  They **could have been** surprised.
  They **may have expected** him to speak longer
  than two minutes.
  They **might have thought** that he wasn't finished.
	We use *may/might/could* + have + past participle to express a possibility about the past.
	They could have been surprised. = *Maybe they were surprised.*
	They may have expected him to say more. = *Maybe they expected* him to say more.

Everett's speech **may not have been** so interesting. Lincoln **might not have realized** how good his speech was.	To show negative possibility, we use *may not have* and *might not have*. We don't use *could not have*, because it has a different meaning. (See Chart 6.8)

EXERCISE 3 Read the words under the blank. Then fill in the blanks to express the same idea with the modal given.

You may ___have learned___ about Abraham Lincoln in school, but here's something you might
   1. maybe you learned

_____. John Wilkes Booth, the man who assassinated Abraham Lincoln, was a
   2. maybe you didn't hear

famous actor. His brother, Edwin, was also an actor. John may _____ as good an
                                                                     3. maybe John was not

actor as his brother, but he was very popular, especially with women. This could

_____ because he was very handsome. John Booth hated the president and was in
   4. maybe this was

favor of slavery. Edwin was on Lincoln's side. John and Edwin argued so much about Lincoln and slavery

that Edwin finally refused to have John in his house. John was planning to harm the president. At first, he

might _____ to kill the president, but later he decided to assassinate him.
         5. maybe he didn't plan

   In a hotel in Pennsylvania, where John Booth often stayed, someone had written these words near a

window: "Abe Lincoln Departed This Life August 13th, 1864 By The Effects of Poison."

   After the death of Lincoln, people thought that John Booth may _____ these
                                                                        6. maybe John Booth wrote

words. But this is not certain. There were many people who hated Lincoln, and someone else could

_____ that sentence.
   7. maybe someone else wrote

   In 1865, Lincoln was attending a play at the Ford Theater in Washington, DC. Booth was not an actor in

that play, but because he had acted there before, no one thought anything of his presence at the theater.

While Lincoln was sitting with his wife watching the play, Booth entered the president's box and shot him

in the head. At first, it was thought that he may _____ Lincoln, but it was soon
                                                     8. maybe he stabbed Lincoln

evident that Booth had shot him. The next morning, Lincoln died.

   There's another interesting story about the Booth brothers. A few months before the assassination,

Robert, Lincoln's son, was standing on a train platform. Just as the train was arriving, Robert fell on the

tracks. It could _____ because of the crowds pushing. A stranger reached out and
                    9. maybe it was

pulled Robert to safety just before the train arrived. This stranger was Edwin Booth, John Wilkes Booth's

brother.

6.4 Logical Conclusion about the Past — *Must Have*

Examples	Explanation
Lincoln had very little schooling. He **must have been** very intelligent to learn so much on his own. I've seen pictures of Lincoln with other people. He looks so tall. He **must have been** over six feet tall.	We use *must have* + past participle to make a logical conclusion, deduction, or estimate about the past. We are saying that something was probably true. *He must have been very intelligent. = He probably was very intelligent.* *He must have been over six feet tall. = I estimate that he was over six feet tall.*
When Lincoln finished his speech after two minutes, some people thought that he **must not have been finished**. Lincoln thought, "They **must not have liked** my speech."	For the negative, we use *must not have* + past participle. We don't use a contraction for *must not*.

EXERCISE 4 Fill in the blanks to express past probability or logical conclusion. Use the underlined verbs and context clues to help you. Answers may vary.

1. **A:** It sounds like Edwin Booth <u>was</u> a kind man.

   B: He risked his life to save Lincoln's son. He must _____*have been*_____ a very kind man.

                                                                    a.

   A: But Edwin's brother, John, was a terrible person.

   B: The brothers must not _____ each other.

                                        b.

   A: It's obvious that they <u>didn't like</u> each other. Edwin didn't even want John in his house.

2. **A:** How did John Booth <u>enter</u> the theater to kill Lincoln?

   B: He must _____ like everyone else. He was a well-known actor, so people didn't think

                            a.

   anything of it.

   A: It's not easy to <u>plan</u> an assassination.

   B: He must _____ the assassination for a long time.

                            b.

   A: Today, presidents <u>have</u> a lot of security. They must not _____ so much security in

                                                                            c.

   Lincoln's time.

3. **A:** Many people loved Lincoln. They must _____ very sad when he died. I <u>felt</u> very sad

                                                    a.

   when I read the story.

   B: But some people hated him. People who wanted to continue slavery must _____

                                                                                    b.

   happy when he died.

continued

4. **A:** Slaves worked so hard. They must _____ a very hard life.
   _{a.}

   B: Yes. They <u>had</u> a very hard life.

   A: The slaves must _____ happy because Lincoln wanted to end slavery.
   _{b.}

   B: I'm sure they <u>were</u> very happy.

5. **A:** Kennedy's death was such a tragedy.

   B: Who's Kennedy?

   A: You never <u>heard</u> of Kennedy? He was so famous. You must _____ of him. There's a
   _{a.}

   picture of him in this book on page 169.

   B: Wow. He <u>was</u> so handsome. He must _____ a movie star.
   _{b.}

   A: No. He <u>was</u> an American president. He was assassinated in 1963 when he was only 46 years old.

   B: That's terrible. It must _____ a hard time for Americans.
   _{c.}

   A: Yes, it <u>was</u>. I remember my grandparents telling me about it.

   B: How old were they at the time?

   A: They <u>were</u> in high school when it happened. They must _____ about fifteen or
   _{d.}

   sixteen years old.

6. **A:** We read about Thomas Jefferson. Wasn't he the president who said "All men are created equal"?

   He must _____ against slavery.
   _{a.}

   B: He <u>wasn't</u> against slavery. Even though he said that, he had a lot of slaves.

7. **A:** Have you ever seen the movie *Lincoln*?

   B: Is it a new movie? Did it just <u>come</u> out?

   A: It's not new. It must _____ out over 10 years ago.
   _{a.}

   B: Was it good? Did you like it?

   A: I thought it was a little boring. I think I missed some of it because I must _____
   _{b.}

   asleep in parts.

   B: I don't think I've ever <u>fallen</u> asleep during a movie.

The CUBAN MISSILE CRISIS

President Kennedy signs the order to block Soviet ships from delivering weapons to Cuba.

Read the following article. Pay special attention to the words in bold.

CD 1
TR 32

It was October and people around the world were terrified. It seemed almost certain that World War III was about to begin, and the planet was in danger of complete destruction. The whole planet? Was this a science fiction story? Unfortunately, no. The danger of worldwide destruction was possible; some thought even probable. "October 27 is a day I'll never forget. The planet **could have been destroyed**," said a former CIA[5] agent. He was referring to October 27, 1962. "It **could have been** the end of the world, but here we are." Forty years later, many of the surviving leaders in this terrifying crisis met to reflect back on the time when their actions **could have resulted** in the end of the world.

Since the 1940s, the United States and the Soviet Union[6] were enemies. The United States discovered that the Soviet Union was beginning to send nuclear missiles to Cuba, which is only about ninety miles from Florida. The American President, John Kennedy, saw this as a direct threat to national security; these weapons **could have been** used to destroy major cities and military bases in the United States. Spy photos showed that missiles in Cuba **could have reached** almost every part of the continental[7] United States in a very short time. On October 22, President Kennedy announced on TV that any attack from Cuba would be considered an attack from the Soviet Union, and he would respond with a full attack on the Soviets. He sent out the U.S. Navy to block Soviet ships from delivering weapons to Cuba. An attack on a U.S. ship **could have grown** into a full nuclear war. This crisis **could have changed** the world as we know it.

Fortunately, diplomacy[8] won over war. The Soviets agreed to send their missiles back and promised to stop building military bases in Cuba. In exchange, the United States promised to remove its missiles from Turkey. What **could have been** a tragic event is now only a chapter in history.

---

5 *CIA:* Central Intelligence Agency. It gathers information about other countries' secrets.

6 The Soviet Union was a country that included Russia, Ukraine, and 13 other republics. In 1991, the government collapsed and the Soviet Union broke up into 15 different countries, the largest of which is Russia.

7 *continental United States:* all U.S. states except Hawaii and Alaska, which are not part of the U.S. mainland

8 *diplomacy:* skillful negotiation between countries to try to work out problems without fighting

COMPREHENSION CHECK Based on the reading, tell if the statement is true (**T**) or false (**F**).

1. Cuba was helping the Soviet Union in 1962.

2. President Kennedy sent ships to attack the Soviet ships.

3. In 2002, leaders met to discuss the decisions they had made in 1962.

6.5 Past Direction Not Taken — *Could Have*

Examples	Explanation
This crisis **could have changed** the world. The planet **could have been destroyed**.	We use *could have* + past participle to show that it was possible for something to happen, but it didn't.
The U.S. **could have attacked** the Soviet ships. The U.S. **could have invaded** Cuba. But the president didn't do these things.	We use *could have* + past participle to show that a past opportunity was not taken.
A: Before we got to class, I didn't know much about Lincoln. B: You **could have read** the article before class. Or you **could have googled** his name.	We use *could have* + past participle to show suggestions that were not followed.

Language Notes:

1. We often use *could have* + past participle in an expression like this: *I was so… I could have…*
   We use this expression to exaggerate a result.

   When the missiles were removed, I was so happy **I could have jumped** for joy.

2. Remember, *could have* + past participle can mean *may have/might have* (maybe). (See Chart 6.3)

EXERCISE 5 Fill in the blanks with *have* + one of the verbs from the box.

sent	started✓	ended	continued
tried	bombed	made	been killed

1. World War III could _____ have started _____ in 1962.

2. In 1962, the world as we know it could _____ .

3. Everyone could _____ .

4. The world leaders could _____ a wrong decision, but they made a sensible decision.

5. The Soviets could _____ to send ships to Cuba, but they stopped.

6. The Soviets could _____ missiles to all the major cities of the U.S. from Cuba.

7. The U.S. could _____ the missile sites in Cuba, but Kennedy decided against that.

8. As the Soviet ships came close to the American naval ships, they could _____ to cross, but they stopped.

EXERCISE 6 Fill in the blanks with *have* + the past participle of one of the verbs from the box.

marry	kill	be	give	dress√	break

1. Lincoln wasn't interested in nice clothes. He could _____ have dressed _____ well, but he usually

   dressed poorly.

2. Lincoln could _____ a farmer like his father, but he wanted to become a lawyer.

3. Mary Todd, Lincoln's wife, was from a wealthy, educated family. Her family thought she could

   _____ a better man than Lincoln. She had other marriage opportunities.

4. The South could _____ away from the North over the issue of slavery, but Lincoln

   saved the nation and kept it together.

5. Lincoln could _____ a long speech, but he decided to give a very short speech.

6. A train could _____ Lincoln's son, but Edwin Booth saved him.

EXERCISE 7 About You Write about a direction you could have taken in your life, but didn't. Discuss your response with a partner.

EXAMPLE: I could have gotten married when I was 18, but I decided to finish college first.

_____

_____

_____

_____

EXERCISE 8 Write about something that almost happened in your country or another country you know about. Use *could have*. Discuss your response with a partner.

EXAMPLE: In Chile, 33 miners were trapped in a mine in 2010. They were there for over

two months. They could have died, but they were saved.

_____

_____

_____

_____

_____

The Media
and PRESIDENTIAL ELECTIONS

🎧 **Read the following article. Pay special attention to the words in bold.**

CD 1
TR 33

There's no doubt about it—the media influence elections. First newspapers, then radio, then television, and now social media—all of these have played an important part in getting out information and shaping public opinion.

One example of how the media **could influence** election results took place in the 1960 presidential race between John Kennedy and Richard Nixon. For the first time in history, two candidates debated[9] each other on TV. John Kennedy was the first candidate who understood the influence that television had on the result of an election. Both candidates **had to answer** difficult questions. Many people who heard the Nixon-Kennedy debate on the radio thought that Nixon was the stronger candidate. But people who saw the debate on TV thought that the young, handsome Kennedy was the better candidate. Also, Nixon was sweating under the hot lights, and people thought that he **must have been** nervous and uncomfortable with the questions. It was a close election, but Kennedy won. Many people think Kennedy **couldn't have won** without TV.

If Kennedy was the first presidential candidate to understand the influence of TV, Barack Obama was the first candidate who understood the influence of social media. For the 2008 election, he reached out to the Internet generation; his opponent, John McCain, didn't even know how to use a computer. He **had to depend** on his wife to read and send e-mail. By the time of the 2012 election between Barack Obama and Mitt Romney, both parties understood the power of social media, but Obama's team **was able to collect** data online and use it more effectively.

When people started to use social media, they no longer **had to get** their information from TV or newspapers or even the Internet. With social media sites, people **could influence** each other. According to a media blog: "In the 2012 election, 30% of online users report that they were urged to vote via social media by family, friends or other social network connections, 20% actively encouraged others, and 22% posted their decision when they voted."

It is clear that political candidates now need social media to get their images and messages across.

John F. Kennedy (left) and Richard Nixon (far right) during their televised presidential debate.

---

[9] *debate:* to answer questions (before an audience) so that the public can judge who is the best candidate

COMPREHENSION CHECK Based on the reading, tell if the statement is true (**T**) or false (**F**).

1. Some of the people who saw Kennedy on TV were influenced by his good looks.

2. Candidates first started getting their message across with TV.

3. People who use social media often influence their friends and family in elections.

6.6 *Must Have* + Past Participle vs. *Had to* + Base Form

Examples	Explanation
Kennedy and Nixon **had to** answer difficult questions. John McCain **had to** depend on his wife to use e-mail.	To show past necessity or obligation, we use *had to* + base form. *Must*, for necessity or obligation, has no past form.
TV viewers thought that Nixon **must have been** nervous and uncomfortable during the debate. John McCain **must not have understood** the importance of social media.	To show a logical conclusion or deduction in the past, we use *must have* + past participle.

EXERCISE 9 Write *had to* + base form for a past necessity. Write *must have* + past participle for a past deduction or logical conclusion.

A: The 2000 election between Al Gore, the Democratic candidate, and George Bush, the Republican

candidate, was so strange.

B: It was?

A: Don't you remember? The election was very close, so they ___had to count___ the votes again to see

                                                            1. count

who won. It took them five weeks to figure out who won the election.

B: Bush and Gore _____ nervous the whole time. They _____

                                  2. be   **3. wait**

a long time to find out the results.

A: This had never happened before. Everyone _____ surprised and confused at that

                                                            4. be

time. There were so many problems counting the votes that the decision _____

                                                                                 5. *passive*: make

by the Supreme Court.

B: Did you vote in that election?

A: Of course. I always vote.

B: You usually vote for a Democrat, so you _____ for Gore.

                                                                  6. vote

A: Yes, I did.

continued

B: You _____ very disappointed when they finally announced that Gore lost.

                          7. be

A: Yes, I was. What about you? Who did you vote for?

B: I _____ overtime that day, so I didn't vote. Anyway, one person's vote doesn't

                     8. work

matter much.

A: It mattered in 2000.

6.7 Ability and Possibility in the Past

Examples	Explanation
President Lincoln **could give** good speeches. He also had a good sense of humor and **was able to make** people laugh.	In affirmative statements, *could* + base form means *used to be able to*. It shows ability or knowledge over a period of time. *Was/were able to* can also be used for ability over a period of time.
In October 1962, President Kennedy **was able to prevent** war. He **was able to convince** the Soviets to send back their missiles.	In affirmative statements, we use *was/were able to* for success in doing a single action. We don't use *could* for a single action.
I **couldn't understand** Lincoln's speech. **Were** you **able to** understand it?	In negative statements and questions, *could* and *was/were able to* are used interchangeably.
The Cuban Missile Crisis **could have destroyed** the world (but it didn't). Lincoln **could have given** a longer speech, but he chose to give a two-minute speech.	We use *could have* + past participle for an action that was possible but didn't happen.
Some people thought that Kennedy **couldn't have won** the election without TV. And maybe Barack Obama **couldn't have won** without social media.	We use *couldn't have* + past participle to show that something was impossible in the past.
A: My grandparents liked to watch President Roosevelt on TV. **B:** They **couldn't have watched** him on TV. They didn't have TV back then. You probably mean radio.	*Couldn't have* + past participle is used to show disbelief or to disprove a previous statement.

EXERCISE 10 Circle the correct words to complete each sentence. In some cases, both choices are possible, so circle both options.

1. I (*couldn't use*/*couldn't have used*) social media last night because I didn't have an Internet connection.

2. We listened to the Gettysburg Address online, but we (*couldn't understand*/*couldn't have understood*) it. The

   vocabulary was difficult for us.

3. Do you mean you listened to Lincoln's voice? You (*couldn't listen*/*couldn't have listened*) to Lincoln's voice. There

   was no recording of his voice. You must have listened to someone else reciting the Gettysburg Address.

4. (*Were you able to/Could you*) vote in the last election?

5. My mother has been a U.S. citizen for the last five years. She (*could vote/could have voted*) in the last election, but she's not interested in politics.

6. Around the time of the 2008 election in the United States, many people (*were able to use/could have used*) social media to get information.

7. You say President Kennedy was killed in a plane crash in 1999. That (*couldn't happen/ couldn't have happened*). He was assassinated in 1963. You're probably thinking of his son.

8. John McCain (*couldn't/wasn't able to*) use social media in 2008.

9. I (*couldn't/wasn't able to*) vote in the last election because I was out of the country.

10. My mother uses social media now. But she (*couldn't use/couldn't have used*) it five years ago. I had to show her how.

11. Lincoln (*could be/could have been*) a farmer like his father, but he was more interested in politics.

12. Lincoln's father (*couldn't read/couldn't have read*).

13. Lincoln (*was able to teach/could have taught*) himself law.

6.8 Modals in the Past: Continuous Forms

Example	Explanation
John Wilkes Booth **must have been** planning the assassination for a long time.	To give a continuous meaning to a past modal, we use modal + *have* + *been* + present participle.

EXERCISE 11 Fill in the blanks with one of the verbs from the box. Use the continuous form.

prepare	think	have	use✓	plan	protect

1. Farmers shouldn't _____ have been using _____ people as slaves.

2. What was Lincoln thinking after his speech? He might _____ about the audience reaction.

3. Lincoln must _____ doubts about his speech.

4. Everett might _____ his speech for several weeks.

5. Lincoln didn't have good protection. Someone should _____ him better.

6. John Booth must _____ the assassination for months.

SUMMARY OF LESSON 6

Examples	Explanation
Lincoln **should have had** better protection. You **should have voted** in the last election. Every vote is important.	We use *should have* + past participle to comment on mistakes or regrets, or to rethink the advisability of a past decision.
In 1962, a nuclear attack was avoided. It **may have been** because of good diplomacy. It **might have been** because the Soviets feared a world war. When John Booth entered the theater, people **could have thought** he was an actor in the play that night.	*May/might/could have* + past participle shows possibility about a past action or event.
People thought Nixon **must have been** nervous because he was sweating. The whole world **must have been** afraid in October 1962.	*Must have* + past participle shows a logical conclusion or deduction about the past.
President Kennedy **could have attacked** the ships, but he didn't. In 1962, a world war **could have started**, but it didn't. You **could have watched** the movie *Lincoln*, but you weren't interested.	*Could have* + past participle shows a past direction not taken, a past possibility that didn't happen, or a past suggestion that wasn't followed.
A: I voted in the last presidential election. B: You **couldn't have voted**. You weren't even 18 at that time.	*Couldn't have* + past participle can show disbelief or an attempt to disprove a previous statement.
When I was younger, I **could name** all the presidents in my country, but now I've forgotten. I **was able to read** Lincolns' speech without using a dictionary.	To express past ability, we use *could* + base form or *was/were able to* + base form. In affirmative statements, *could* means *used to be able to*. To show success in doing a single action, we use *was/were able to* for affirmative statements.
McCain didn't know how to use a computer. He **had to depend** on his wife.	*Had to* + base form shows an obligation or necessity in the past.
Booth **must have been planning** the assassination for some time.	For a continuous meaning of a past modal, we use modal + *have* + *been* + present participle.

TEST/REVIEW

Circle the correct words to complete each conversation. If both choices are possible, circle both.

1. **A:** Our grandparents (*had to rely*/*should have relied*) on TV or newspapers to get the news.
   a.

   B: I can't imagine a time without social media. Getting the news (*must*/*should*) have been so slow.
   b.

2. **A:** Did you read the article about Lincoln last night?

   B: I (*couldn't read*/*couldn't have read*) it. I didn't have time. What about you?
   a.

   A: I (*was able to*/*could*) read it, but I (*wasn't able to*/*couldn't*) understand every word.
   b.   **c.**

3. **A:** Without Lincoln, slavery (*should*/*could*) have lasted much longer.
   a.

   B: Lincoln (*was able to end*/*could have ended*) slavery and keep the country together.
   b.

4. **A:** Lincoln's bodyguard (*couldn't*/*shouldn't*) have left the president alone. Where was he?
   a.

   B: I'm not sure. He (*might not*/*should not*) have been in the theater with Lincoln.
   b.

5. **A:** After Booth shot Lincoln, he jumped onto the stage.

   B: The audience (*had to think*/*must have thought*) this was part of the play.
   a.

6. **A:** Did they take Lincoln back to the White House?

   B: It was too far. They (*had to take*/*must have taken*) him to a house across the street. He died there the
   a.
   next morning.

7. **A:** When Lincoln died, the Secretary of War said something interesting, but people

   (*couldn't have agreed*/*weren't able to agree*) on what he said.
   a.

   B: Yes. He (*may*/*might*) have said, "Now he belongs to the ages" or he (*could*/*may*) have said, "Now he
   b.   **c.**
   belongs to the angels."

8. **A:** When John Kennedy was president, a world war (*could happen*/*could have happened*), but it didn't.
   a.
   He had to make some difficult decisions.

   B: He (*could*/*must*) have made the right decision back then. He prevented a war.
   b.

9. **A:** Kennedy was another president who was assassinated. Who killed him?

   B: We don't know for sure. It (*may*/*might*) have been the Soviets. The assassination (*must*/*could*) have
   a.   **b.**
   been prevented. He was in an open car. He (*should*/*must*) have had better protection.
   c.

WRITING

PART 1 Editing Advice

1. After a modal, always use a base form.

   Lincoln should ~~has~~ *have* had more protection.

2. To express the past with some modals, use modal + *have* + past participle.

   The bodyguard shouldn't ∧*have* left the theater.

3. Don't use *of* after a modal to express past. Use the auxiliary verb *have*.

   The Cuban Missile Crisis could ~~of~~ *have* caused a third world war.

4. Use the correct form for the past participle.

   Lincoln shouldn't have ~~went~~ *gone* to the theater that night.

5. *Can* is never used for the past.

   I ~~can't voted~~ *couldn't vote* in the last election.

6. Don't confuse *couldn't have* + past participle with *couldn't* + base form.

   When we read the article about Lincoln, I couldn't ~~have understood~~ *understand* a few words.

   If you didn't understand the article, you could ∧*have* use∧*d* a dictionary.

PART 2 Editing Practice

Some of the shaded words and phrases have mistakes. Find the mistakes and correct them. If the shaded words are correct, write C.

You probably know about the assassination of President Kennedy. But do you know about the

tragic death of his son in 1999?

John Junior was less than three years old when his father was killed. Because he was so young,

he can't remembered *couldn't remember* much about father. But of course he must have known *C* a lot about his father
     1.   **2.**

from his family and from history. And he must remembered his uncle Robert, who was assassinated
                                       3.

when John was eight years old.

John Junior could be a politician like his dad and uncles. He might have been discouraged from
          4.   **5.**

going into politics because both his father and uncle Robert were assassinated. Instead he became a

lawyer. After a few years as a lawyer, he decided to publish a political magazine. So he must of been
                                                                                        6.

interested in politics.

Because he was so famous, he couldn't go out in public without being followed by photographers.
                                 7.
When he flew on commercial airlines, other passengers asked him questions, took his picture, and
wanted his autograph. He can't got any privacy at all. So he decided to get his pilot's license and fly
                              8.
his own airplane.

Only fifteen months after getting his license, he planned to fly with his wife to his cousin's
wedding in Massachusetts. They were supposed to be there after a short flight. Family members
waited and waited. They couldn't have understood why John didn't arrive on time. After waiting all
                           9.
night with no word from John, they must knew that something terrible had happened.
                                 10.
The following morning, searchers found their suitcases on the shore. They concluded that the
plane must has crashed. Families members couldn't go on with the wedding. Six days later, the
       11.   12.
bodies were found.

Experts tried to understand the reason for the crash. John didn't have a lot of experience as a
pilot and flew over water, which is difficult for new pilots. Experts say he should have flew over land.
                                                                      13.
Also, the weather wasn't good that evening. So he should have waited. He had broken his ankle a few
                                              14.
months before. Some people think he may not been able to handle the foot pedals of the airplane.
                                    15.
This tragedy could be prevented. He could of used a commercial airline. Or he could have hired
                16.   17.   18.
a professional pilot to take him there in his own airplane.

John Kennedy, Jr. was only 38 years old. This was just one more tragedy for the Kennedy family.

PART 3 Write About It

1. Write about an event that had a big impact on the U.S., your country, or the world. Or write about a tragedy that was avoided. Provide the sources you used to write your essay.

2. Write about the tragic death of a famous person. Provide the sources you used to write your essay.

PART 4 Edit Your Writing

Reread the Summary of Lesson 6 and the editing advice. Edit your writing from Part 3.

Vowel and Consonant Pronunciation Charts

Vowels

Symbol	Examples
ʌ	love, cup
a	father, box
æ	class, black
ə	alone, atom
ɛ	ever, well
i	eat, feet
ɪ	miss, bit
ɔ	talk, corn
ʊ	would, book
oʊ	cone, boat
u	tooth, through
eɪ	able, day
aɪ	mine, try
aʊ	about, cow
ɔɪ	join, boy

Consonants

Symbol	Examples
b	bread, cab
d	door, dude
f	form, if
g	go, flag
h	hello, behind
j	use, yellow
k	cook, hike
l	leg, little
m	month, time
n	never, nine
ŋ	singer, walking
p	put, map
r	river, try
s	saw, parks
ʃ	show, action
ɾ	atom, lady
t	take, tent
tʃ	check, church
θ	thing, both
ð	the, either
v	voice, of
w	would, reward
z	zoo, mazes
ʒ	usual, vision
dʒ	just, edge

Noncount Nouns

There are several types of noncount nouns.

Group A: Nouns that have no distinct, separate parts. We look at the whole.			
milk	yogurt	paper	cholesterol
oil	poultry	rain	blood
water	bread	air	
coffee	meat	electricity	
tea	soup	lightning	
juice	butter	thunder	

Group B: Nouns that have parts that are too small or insignificant to count.			
rice	hair	sand	
sugar	popcorn	corn	
salt	snow	grass	

Group C: Nouns that are classes or categories of things. The members of the category are not the same.	
money or cash (nickels, dimes, dollars)	mail (letters, packages, postcards, flyers)
furniture (chairs, tables, beds)	homework (compositions, exercises, readings)
clothing (sweaters, pants, dresses)	jewelry (necklaces, bracelets, rings)

Group D: Nouns that are abstractions.					
love	happiness	nutrition	patience	work	nature
truth	education	intelligence	poverty	health	help
beauty	advice	unemployment	music	fun	energy
luck/fortune	knowledge	pollution	art	information	friendship

Group E: Subjects of study.		
history	grammar	biology
chemistry	geometry	math (mathematics*)

*Note: Even though *mathematics* ends with *s*, it is not plural.

continued

Notice the quantity words used with count and noncount nouns.

Singular Count	Plural Count	Noncount
a tomato	tomatoes	coffee
one tomato	**two** tomatoes	**two cups of** coffee
	some tomatoes	**some** coffee
no tomato	**no** tomatoes	**no** coffee
	any tomatoes (with questions and negatives)	**any** coffee (with questions and negatives)
	a lot of tomatoes	**a lot of** coffee
	many tomatoes	**much** coffee (with questions and negatives)
	a few tomatoes	**a little** coffee
	several tomatoes	**several** cups of coffee
	How many tomatoes?	**How much** coffee?

The following words can be used as either count nouns or noncount nouns. However, the meaning changes according to the way the nouns are used.

Count	Noncount
Oranges and grapefruit are **fruits** that contain a lot of vitamin C.	I bought some **fruit** at the fruit store.
Ice cream and butter are **foods** that contain cholesterol.	We don't need to go shopping today. We have a lot of **food** at home.
He wrote a **paper** about hypnosis.	I need some **paper** to write my composition.
He committed three **crimes** last year.	There is a lot of **crime** in a big city.
I have two hundred **chickens** on my farm.	We ate some **chicken** for dinner.
I don't want to bore you with all my **troubles.**	I have some **trouble** with my car.
She went to Puerto Rico three **times.**	She spent a lot of **time** on her project.
She drank three **glasses** of water.	The window is made of bulletproof **glass.**
I had a bad **experience** during my trip to Paris.	She has some **experience** with computer programming.
I don't know much about the **lives** of my grandparents.	**Life** is sometimes happy, sometimes sad.
I heard a **noise** outside my window.	Those children are making a lot of **noise.**

Use of Articles

PART 1 Use of the Indefinite Article

A. To classify a subject

Examples	Explanation
Chicago is **a** city. Illinois is **a** state. Abraham Lincoln was **an** American president.	• We use *a* before a consonant sound. • We use *an* before a vowel sound. • We can put an adjective before the noun.
Chicago and Los Angeles are cities. Lincoln and Washington were American presidents.	We do not use an article before a plural noun.

B. To make a generalization about a noun

Examples	Explanation
A dog has sharp teeth. **Dogs** have sharp teeth. **An elephant** has big ears. **Elephants** have big ears.	We use an indefinite article *(a/an)* + a singular count noun or no article with a plural noun. Both the singular and plural forms have the same meaning.
Coffee contains caffeine. **Love** makes people happy.	We do not use an article to make a generalization about a noncount noun.

C. To introduce a new noun into the conversation

Examples	Explanation
I have **a cell phone**. I have **an umbrella**.	We use the indefinite article *a/an* with singular count nouns.
I have **(some) dishes**. Do you have **(any) cups**? I don't have **(any) forks**. I have **(some) money** with me. Do you have **(any) cash** with you? I don't have **(any) time**.	We use *some* or *any* with plural nouns and noncount nouns. We use *any* in questions and negatives. *Some* and *any* can be omitted.
There's **an elevator** in the building. There isn't **any money** in my wallet.	*There* + a form of *be* can introduce an indefinite noun into a conversation.

continued

PART 2 Use of the Definite Article

A. To refer to a previously mentioned noun

Examples	Explanation
There's **a dog** in the next apartment. **The dog** barks all the time.	We start by saying *a dog*. We continue by saying *the dog*.
We bought **some grapes.** We ate **the grapes** this morning.	We start by saying *some grapes.* We continue by saying *the grapes.*
I need **some sugar.** I'm going to use **the sugar** to bake a cake.	We start by saying *some sugar.* We continue by saying *the sugar.*
Did you buy **any coffee?** Yes. **The coffee** is in the cabinet.	We start by saying *any coffee.* We continue by saying *the coffee.*

B. When the speaker and the listener have the same reference

Examples	Explanation
The number on this page is AP5.	The object is present, so the speaker and listener have the same object in mind.
The president is talking about **the** economy.	People who live in the same country have things in common.
Please turn off **the lights** and shut **the door** before you leave **the house.**	People who live in the same house have things in common.
The house on the corner is beautiful. I spent **the money you gave me.**	The listener knows exactly which one because the speaker defines or specifies which one.

C. When there is only one in our experience

Examples	Explanation
The sun is bigger than **the moon.** There are many problems in **the world.**	The *sun*, the *moon*, and the *world* are unique objects.
Write your name on **the top** of the page.	The page has only one top.
Alaska is **the biggest** state in the U.S.	A superlative indicates that there is only one.

D. With familiar places

Examples	Explanation
I'm going to **the store** after work. Do you need anything? **The bank** is closed now. I'll go tomorrow.	We use *the* with certain familiar places and people—*the bank, the zoo, the park, the store, the movies, the beach, the post office, the bus, the train, the doctor, the dentist*—when we refer to the one that we habitually visit or use.

Language Notes:

1. Omit *the* after a preposition with the words *church, school, work,* and *bed.*

He's **in church.**   They're **at work.**
I'm going **to school.**   I'm going **to bed.**

2. Omit *to* and *the* with *home* and *downtown.*

I'm going **home.**   Are you going **downtown** after class?

continued

E. To make a formal generalization

Examples	Explanation
The shark is the oldest and most primitive fish.	To say that something is true of all members of a group, use *the* with singular count nouns.
The computer has changed the way people deal with information.	To talk about a class of inventions, use *the*.
The ear has three parts: outer, middle, and inner.	To talk about an organ of the body in a general sense, use *the*.
Language Note:	

For informal generalizations, use *a* + a singular noun or no article with a plural noun.
>   **The computer** has changed the way we deal with information. (Formal)
>   **A computer** is expensive. (Informal)
>   **Computers** are expensive. (Informal)

PART 3   Special Uses of Articles

No Article	Article

Personal names:
    John Kennedy
	The whole family:
	    the Kennedys

Title and name:
    Queen Elizabeth
	Title without name:
	    the Queen

Cities, states, countries, continents:
    Cleveland
    Ohio
    Mexico
    South America
	Places that are considered a union:
	    the United States
	Place names: the _____ of _____
	    the District of Columbia

Mountains:
    Mount Everest
	Mountain ranges:
	    the Rocky Mountains

Islands:
    Staten Island
	Collectives of islands:
	    the Hawaiian Islands

Lakes:
    Lake Superior
	Collectives of lakes:
	    the Great Lakes

Beaches:
    Palm Beach
    Pebble Beach
	Rivers, oceans, seas:
	    the Mississippi River
	    the Atlantic Ocean
	    the Dead Sea

Streets and avenues:
    Madison Avenue
    Wall Street
	Well-known buildings:
	    the Willis Tower
	    the Empire State Building

Parks:
    Central Park
	Zoos:
	    the San Diego Zoo

No Article	Article

Seasons:
    summer   fall   spring   winter
    Summer is my favorite season.
 	
    Note: After a preposition, *the* may be used.
    In (the) winter, my car runs badly.
	Deserts:
	    the Mojave Desert
	    the Sahara Desert

Directions:
    north   south   east   west
	Sections of a piece of land:
	    the West Side (of New York)

School subjects:
    history   math
	Unique geographical points:
	    the North Pole the Vatican

Name + *college* or *university*:
    Northwestern University
	The University/College of _____
	    the University of Michigan

Magazines:
    Time   *Sports Illustrated*
	Newspapers:
	    the *Tribune* the *Wall Street Journal*

Months and days:
    September   Monday
	Ships:
	    the *Titanic* the *Queen Elizabeth II*

Holidays and dates:
    Mother's Day
    July 4 (month + day)
	The day of month:
	    the fifth of May
	    the Fourth of July

Diseases:
    cancer   AIDS
    polio   malaria
	Ailments:
	    a cold a toothache
	    a headache the flu

Games and sports:
    poker
    soccer
	Musical instruments, after *play*:
	    the drums the piano
	Note: Sometimes *the* is omitted.
	    She plays (the) drums.

Languages:
    English
	The _____ language:
	    the English language

Last month, year, week, etc. = the one before this one:
    I forgot to pay my rent last month.
    The teacher gave us a test last week.
	The last month, the last year, the last week, etc. = the last in a series:
	    December is the last month of the year.
	    Vacation begins the last week in May.

In office = in an elected position:
    The president is in office for four years.
	In the office = in a specific room:
	    The teacher is in the office.

In back/in front:
    She's in back
    of the car.
	In the back/in the front:
	    He's in the back of the bus.

Verbs and Adjectives Followed by a Preposition

Many verbs and adjectives are followed by a preposition.

accuse someone of	(be) familiar with	(be) prepared for/to
(be) accustomed to	(be) famous for	prevent (someone) from
adjust to	(be) fond of	prohibit (someone) from
(be) afraid of	forget about	protect (someone) from
agree with	forgive someone for	(be) proud of
(be) amazed at/by	(be) glad about	recover from
(be) angry about	(be) good at	(be) related to
(be) angry at/with	(be) grateful to someone for	rely on/upon
apologize for	(be) guilty of	(be) responsible for
approve of	(be) happy about	(be) sad about
argue about	hear about	(be) satisfied with
argue with	hear of	(be) scared of
(be) ashamed of	hope for	(be) sick of
(be) aware of	(be) incapable of	(be) sorry about
believe in	insist on/upon	(be) sorry for
blame someone for	(be) interested in	speak about
(be) bored with/by	(be) involved in	speak to/with
(be) capable of	(be) jealous of	succeed in
care about	(be) known for	(be) sure of/about
care for	(be) lazy about	(be) surprised at
compare to/with	listen to	take care of
complain about	look at	talk about
concentrate on	look for	talk to/with
(be) concerned about	look forward to	thank (someone) for
consist of	(be) mad about	(be) thankful (to someone) for
count on	(be) mad at	think about/of
deal with	(be) made from/of	(be) tired of
decide on	(be) married to	(be) upset about
depend on/upon	object to	(be) upset with
(be) different from	(be) opposed to	(be) used to
disapprove of	participate in	wait for
(be) divorced from	plan on	warn (someone) about
dream about/of	pray to	(be) worried about
(be) engaged to	pray for	worry about
(be) excited about		

Direct and Indirect Objects

<table>
<tr><td colspan="2">The order of direct and indirect objects depends on the verb we use. It also can depend on whether we use a noun or a pronoun as the object.</td></tr>
</table>

Group 1	Pronouns affect word order. The preposition used is *to*.
Patterns:	He gave a present to his wife. (DO to IO)
	He gave his wife a present. (IO/DO)
	He gave it to his wife. (DO to IO)
	He gave her a present. (IO/DO)
	He gave it to her. (DO to IO)

Verbs:	bring	lend	pass	sell	show	teach
	give	offer	pay	send	sing	tell
	hand	owe	read	serve	take	write

Group 2	Pronouns affect word order. The preposition used is *for*.
Patterns:	He bought a car for his daughter. (DO for IO)
	He bought his daughter a car. (IO/DO)
	He bought it for his daughter. (DO for IO)
	He bought her a car. (IO/DO)
	He bought it for her. (DO for IO)

Verbs:	bake	buy	draw	get	make
	build	do	find	knit	reserve

Group 3	Pronouns don't affect word order. The preposition used is *to*.
Patterns:	He explained the problem to his friend. (DO to IO)
	He explained it to her. (DO to IO)

Verbs:	admit	explain	prove	report	say
	announce	introduce	recommend	speak	
	describe	mention	repeat	suggest	

Group 4	Pronouns don't affect word order. The preposition used is *for*.
Patterns:	He cashed a check for his friend. (DO for IO)
	He cashed it for her. (DO for IO)

Verbs:	answer	change	design	open	prescribe
	cash	close	fix	prepare	pronounce

Group 5	Pronouns don't affect word order. No preposition is used.
Patterns:	She asked the teacher a question. (IO/DO)
	She asked him a question. (IO/DO)

Verbs:	ask	charge	cost	wish	take (with time)

Plural Forms of Nouns

Irregular Noun Plurals		
Singular	**Plural**	**Explanation**
man woman tooth foot goose	men women teeth feet geese	Vowel change (**Note:** The first vowel in *women* is pronounced /ɪ/.)
sheep fish deer	sheep fish deer	No change
child person mouse	children people (OR persons) mice	Different word form
alumnus cactus radius stimulus syllabus	alumni cacti (OR cactuses) radii stimuli syllabi (OR syllabuses)	*us → i*
analysis crisis hypothesis oasis parenthesis thesis	analyses crises hypotheses oases parentheses theses	*is → es*
appendix index	appendices (OR appendixes) indices (OR indexes)	*ix → ices* OR *→ ixes* *ex → ices* OR *→ exes*
bacterium curriculum datum medium memorandum criterion phenomenon	bacteria curricula data media memoranda criteria phenomena	*um → a* *ion → a* *on → a*
alga formula vertebra	algae formulae (OR formulas) vertebrae	*a → ae*

Metric Conversion Chart

Length

When You Know	Multiply by	To Find
inches (in)	2.54	centimeters (cm)
feet (ft)	30.5	centimeters (cm)
feet (ft)	0.3	meters (m)
miles (mi)	1.6	kilometers (km)
Metric:		
centimeters (cm)	0.39	inches (in)
centimeters (cm)	0.03	feet (ft)
meters (m)	3.28	feet (ft)
kilometers (km)	0.62	miles (mi)
Note: 12 inches = 1 foot 3 feet = 36 inches = 1 yard		

Weight (Mass)

When You Know	Multiply by	To Find
ounces (oz)	28.35	grams (g)
pounds (lb)	0.45	kilograms (kg)
Metric:		
grams (g)	0.04	ounces (oz)
kilograms (kg)	2.2	pounds (lb)
Note: 1 pound = 16 ounces		

continued

Volume

When You Know	Multiply by	To Find
fluid ounces (fl oz)	30.0	milliliters (mL)
pints (pt)	0.47	liters (L)
quarts (qt)	0.95	liters (L)
gallons (gal)	3.8	liters (L)
Metric:		
milliliters (mL)	0.03	fluid ounces (fl oz)
liters (L)	2.11	pints (pt)
liters (L)	1.05	quarts (qt)
liters (L)	0.26	gallons (gal)
Note: 1 pint = 2 cups 1 quart = 2 pints = 4 cups 1 gallon = 4 quarts = 8 pints = 16 cups		

Temperature

When You Know	Do this	To Find
degrees Fahrenheit (°F)	Subtract 32, then multiply by $5/9$	degrees Celsius (°C)
Metric:		
degrees Celsius (°C)	Multiply by $9/5$, then add 32	degrees Fahrenheit (°F)
Note: 32°F = 0°C 212°F = 100°C		

Irregular Verb Forms

Base Form	Past Form	Past Participle	Base Form	Past Form	Past Participle
be	was/were	been	find	found	found
bear	bore	born/borne	fit	fit	fit
beat	beat	beaten	flee	fled	fled
become	became	become	fly	flew	flown
begin	began	begun	forbid	forbade	forbidden
bend	bent	bent	forget	forgot	forgotten
bet	bet	bet	forgive	forgave	forgiven
bid	bid	bid	freeze	froze	frozen
bind	bound	bound	get	got	gotten
bite	bit	bitten	give	gave	given
bleed	bled	bled	go	went	gone
blow	blew	blown	grind	ground	ground
break	broke	broken	grow	grew	grown
breed	bred	bred	hang	hung	hung
bring	brought	brought	have	had	had
broadcast	broadcast	broadcast	hear	heard	heard
build	built	built	hide	hid	hidden
burst	burst	burst	hit	hit	hit
buy	bought	bought	hold	held	held
cast	cast	cast	hurt	hurt	hurt
catch	caught	caught	keep	kept	kept
choose	chose	chosen	know	knew	known
cling	clung	clung	lay	laid	laid
come	came	come	lead	led	led
cost	cost	cost	leave	left	left
creep	crept	crept	lend	lent	lent
cut	cut	cut	let	let	let
deal	dealt	dealt	lie	lay	lain
dig	dug	dug	light	lit/lighted	lit/lighted
dive	dove/dived	dove/dived	lose	lost	lost
do	did	done	make	made	made
draw	drew	drawn	mean	meant	meant
drink	drank	drunk	meet	met	met
drive	drove	driven	mistake	mistook	mistaken
eat	ate	eaten	overcome	overcame	overcome
fall	fell	fallen	overdo	overdid	overdone
feed	fed	fed	overtake	overtook	overtaken
feel	felt	felt	overthrow	overthrew	overthrown
fight	fought	fought	pay	paid	paid

continued

Base Form	Past Form	Past Participle	Base Form	Past Form	Past Participle
plead	pled/pleaded	pled/pleaded	sting	stung	stung
prove	proved	proven/proved	stink	stank	stunk
put	put	put	strike	struck	struck/stricken
quit	quit	quit	strive	strove	striven
read	read	read	swear	swore	sworn
ride	rode	ridden	sweep	swept	swept
ring	rang	rung	swell	swelled	swelled/swollen
rise	rose	risen	swim	swam	swum
run	ran	run	swing	swung	swung
say	said	said	take	took	taken
see	saw	seen	teach	taught	taught
seek	sought	sought	tear	tore	torn
sell	sold	sold	tell	told	told
send	sent	sent	think	thought	thought
set	set	set	throw	threw	thrown
sew	sewed	sewn/sewed	understand	understood	understood
shake	shook	shaken	uphold	upheld	upheld
shed	shed	shed	upset	upset	upset
shine	shone/shined	shone/shined	wake	woke	woken
shoot	shot	shot	wear	wore	worn
show	showed	shown/showed	weave	wove	woven
shrink	shrank/shrunk	shrunk/shrunken	wed	wedded/wed	wedded/wed
shut	shut	shut	weep	wept	wept
sing	sang	sung	win	won	won
sink	sank	sunk	wind	wound	wound
sit	sat	sat	withdraw	withdrew	withdrawn
sleep	slept	slept	withhold	withheld	withheld
slide	slid	slid	withstand	withstood	withstood
slit	slit	slit	wring	wrung	wrung
speak	spoke	spoken	write	wrote	written
speed	sped	sped			
spend	spent	spent			
spin	spun	spun			
spit	spit/spat	spit/spat			
split	split	split			
spread	spread	spread			
spring	sprang	sprung			
stand	stood	stood			
steal	stole	stolen			
stick	stuck	stuck			

Note:

The past and past participle of some verbs can end in -ed or -t.

burn	burned or burnt
dream	dreamed or dreamt
kneel	kneeled or knelt
learn	learned or learnt
leap	leaped or leapt
spill	spilled or spilt
spoil	spoiled or spoilt

Map of the United States of America

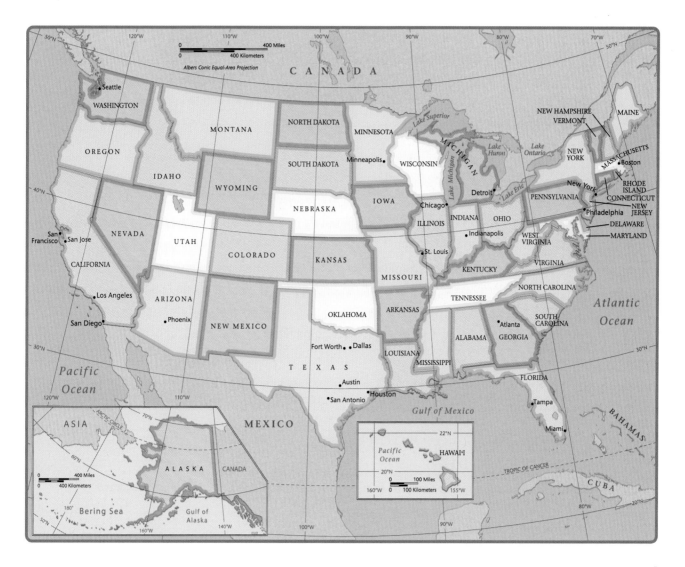

- **Adjective** An adjective gives a description of a noun.

    It's a *tall* tree.   He's an *old* man.   My neighbors are *nice*.

- **Adverb** An adverb describes the action of a sentence or an adjective or another adverb.

    She speaks English *fluently*.   I drive *carefully*.

    She speaks English *extremely* well.   She is *very* intelligent.

- **Adverb of Frequency** An adverb of frequency tells how often an action happens.

    I *never* drink coffee.   They *usually* take the bus.

- **Affirmative** *Affirmative* means "yes."

    They *live* in Miami.

- **Apostrophe** ' We use the apostrophe for possession and contractions.

    My *sister's* friend is beautiful. (possession)

    Today *isn't* Sunday. (contraction)

- **Article** An article comes before a noun. It tells if the noun is definite or indefinite. The definite article is *the*. The indefinite articles are *a* and *an*.

    I have *a* cat.   I ate *an* apple.   *The* teacher came late.

- **Auxiliary Verb** An auxiliary verb is used in forming tense, mood, or aspect of the verb that follows it. Some verbs have two parts: an auxiliary verb and a main verb.

    You *didn't* eat lunch.   He *can't* study.   We *will* return.

- **Base Form** The base form of the verb has no tense. It has no ending (*-s* or *-ed*): *be, go, eat, take, write*.

    I didn't *go*.   We don't *know* you.   He can't *drive*.

- **Capital Letter** A B C D E F G . . .

- **Clause** A clause is a group of words that has a subject and a verb. Some sentences have only one clause.

    She speaks Spanish.

Some sentences have a **main clause** and a **dependent clause**.

MAIN CLAUSE	DEPENDENT CLAUSE (**reason clause**)
She found a good job	because she has computer skills.

MAIN CLAUSE	DEPENDENT CLAUSE (**time clause**)
She'll turn off the light	before she goes to bed.

MAIN CLAUSE	DEPENDENT CLAUSE (***if* clause**)
I'll take you to the doctor	if you don't have your car on Saturday.

- **Colon** :

- **Comma** ,

- **Comparative** The comparative form of an adjective or adverb is used to compare two things.

  My house is *bigger* than your house.

  Her husband drives *faster* than she does.

  My children speak English *more fluently* than I do.

- **Consonant** The following letters are consonants: *b, c, d, f, g, h, j, k, l, m, n, p, q, r, s, t, v, w, x, y, z.*

  NOTE: *Y* is sometimes considered a vowel, as in the world *syllable.*

- **Contraction** A contraction is two words joined with an apostrophe.

  He's my brother.   *You're* late.   They *won't* talk to me.

  (*He's = he is*)   (*You're = you are*)   (*won't = will not*)

- **Count Noun** Count nouns are nouns that we can count. They have a singular and a plural form.

  1 pen–3 pens   1 table–4 tables

- **Dependent Clause** See **Clause**.

- **Direct Object** A direct object is a noun (phrase) or pronoun that receives the action of the verb.

  We saw *the movie.*   You have *a nice car.*   I love *you.*

- **Exclamation Mark** !

- **Frequency Word** Frequency words (*always, usually, generally, often, sometimes, rarely, seldom, hardly ever, never.*) tell how often an action happens.

  I *never* drink coffee.   We *always* do our homework.

- **Hyphen** -

- **Imperative** An imperative sentence gives a command or instructions. An imperative sentence omits the subject pronoun *you.*

  Come here.   *Don't be* late.   Please *help* me.

- **Infinitive** An infinitive is *to* + the base form.

  I want to *leave.*   You need *to be* here on time.

- **Linking Verb** A linking verb is a verb that links the subject to the noun, adjective, or adverb after it. Linking verbs include *be, seem, feel, smell, sound, look, appear,* and *taste.*

  She *is* a doctor.   She *looks* tired.   You *are* late.

- **Main Clause** See **Clause**.

- **Modal** The modal verbs are *can, could, shall, should, will, would, may, might,* and *must.*

    They *should* leave.   I *must* go.

- **Negative** *Negative* means "no."

- **Nonaction Verb** A nonaction verb has no action. We do not use a continuous tense (*be* + verb *-ing*) with a nonaction verb. The nonaction verbs are: *believe, cost, care, have, hear, know, like, love, matter, mean, need, own, prefer, remember, see, seem, think, understand, want,* and sense-perception verbs.

    She *has* a laptop.   We *love* our mother.   You *look* great.

- **Noncount Noun** A noncount noun is a noun that we don't count. It has no plural form.

    She drank some *water.*   He prepared some *rice.*

    Do you need any *money*?   We had a lot of *homework.*

- **Noun** A noun is a person, a place, or a thing. Nouns can be either count or noncount.

    My *brother* lives in California.   My *sisters* live in New York.

    I get *advice* from them.   I drink *coffee* every day.

- **Noun Modifier** A noun modifier makes a noun more specific.

    fire department   *Independence* Day   *can* opener

- **Noun Phrase** A noun phrase is a group of words that form the subject or object of the sentence.

    A very nice woman helped me.   I bought *a big box of cereal.*

- **Object** The object of the sentence follows the verb. It receives the action of the verb.

    He bought *a car.*   I saw *a movie.*   I met *your brother.*

- **Object Pronoun** We use object pronouns (*me, you, him, her, it, us, them*) after the verb or preposition.

    He likes *her.*   I saw the movie. Let's talk about *it.*

- **Parentheses** ( )

- **Paragraph** A paragraph is a group of sentences about one topic.

- **Past Participle** The past participle of a verb is the third form of the verb.

    You have *written* a good essay.   I was *told* about the concert.

- **Period** .

- **Phrasal Modal** Phrasal modals, such as *ought to, be able to,* are made up of two or more words.

    You *ought to* study more.   We *have to* take a test.

- **Phrase** A group of words that go together.

    Last month my sister came to visit.   There is a strange car *in front of my house.*

- **Plural** *Plural* means "more than one." A plural noun usually ends with *-s.*

    She has beautiful *eyes.*   My *feet* are big.

- **Possessive Form** Possessive forms show ownership or relationship.

  Mary's coat is in the closet.   *My* brother lives in Miami.

- **Preposition** A preposition is a short connecting word. Some common prepositions include *about, above, across, after, around, as, at, away, back, before, behind, below, by, down, for, from, in, into, like, of, off, on, out, over, to, under, up,* and *with.*

  The book is *on* the table.   She studies *with* her friends.

- **Present Participle** The present participle of a verb is the base form + *-ing.*

  She is *sleeping.*   They were *laughing.*

- **Pronoun** A pronoun takes the place of a noun.

  I have a new car. I bought *it* last week.

  John likes Mary, but *she* doesn't like *him.*

- **Punctuation** The use of specific marks, such as commas and periods, to make ideas within writing clear.

- **Question Mark** ?

- **Quotation Marks** " "

- **Regular Verb** A regular verb forms its past tense with *-ed.*

  He *worked* yesterday.   I *laughed* at the joke.

- **-s Form** A present tense verb that ends in *-s* or *-es.*

  He *lives* in New York.   She *watches* TV a lot.

- **Sense-Perception Verb** A sense-perception verb has no action. It describes a sense. The sense-perception verbs are: *look, feel, taste, sound,* and *smell.*

  She *feels* fine.   The coffee *smells* fresh.   The milk *tastes* sour.

- **Sentence** A sentence is a group of words that contains a subject and a verb and gives a complete thought.

  SENTENCE: She came home.

  NOT A SENTENCE: When she came home

- **Singular** *Singular* means "one."

  She ate a *sandwich.*   I have one *television.*

- **Subject** The subject of the sentence tells who or what the sentence is about.

  My sister got married last April. *The wedding* was beautiful.

- **Subject Pronoun** We use a subject pronoun (*I, you, he, she, it, we, you, they*) before a verb.

    They speak Japanese.   *We* speak Spanish.

- **Superlative** The superlative form of an adjective or adverb shows the number one item in a group of three or more.

    January is the *coldest* month of the year.

    My brother speaks English the *best* in my family.

- **Syllable** A syllable is a part of a word. Each syllable has only one vowel sound. (Some words have only one syllable.)

    change (one syllable)   after (af·ter = two syllables)

    look (one syllable)   responsible (re·spon·si·ble = four syllables)

- **Tag Question** A tag question is a short question at the end of a sentence. It is used in conversation.

    You speak Spanish, *don't you*?   He's not happy, *is he*?

- **Tense** Tense shows when the action of the sentence happened. Verbs have different tenses.

    SIMPLE PRESENT: She usually *works* hard.

    PRESENT CONTINUOUS: She *is working* now.

    SIMPLE PAST: She *worked* yesterday.

    FUTURE: She *will work* tomorrow.

- **Verb** A verb is the action of the sentence.

    He *runs* fast.   I *speak* English.

- **Vowel** The following letters are vowels: *a, e, i, o, u.*

    NOTE: *Y* is sometimes considered a vowel, as in the world *syllable.*

INDEX

Note: All page references in blue are in Split Edition A.

PHOTOGRAPHIC CREDITS